ENDORSEMENTS

for IN THE COUNSEL OF ANGELS

My husband and I have known Bob Blase for many years as a friend and co-laborer in the kingdom of God. We first met in the early 70's in Alaska where we lived and were actively seeking to know the Lord together. Bob moves in the prophetic realm and his new book, *In the Counsel of Angels*, is a testament of his relationship with the Lord. It opens up a window into the ministry of the angelic host, God's messengers, who do His bidding. I found it inspired me to stay alert to what is happening in the spiritual realm and to have my ears tuned into what God is saying in this hour.

- Rev. Nancy M. Campbell, White Fields Church, Wasilla, Alaska

・・・・・・・・・・

Bob Blase's book, *In the Counsel of Angels*, draws you into largely unexplored realms of angelic encounters and their personal and corporate activity with God's people. This book will awaken you to what is happening in the unseen realm and how we can respond. As you read about Bob's personal encounters with the angelic, you will be compelled to join into a greater partnership with these servants of the Lord. God has hosts of angels all around us just waiting to partner with us in

seeing the glory of the Lord fill the whole earth.
- Kathi Pelton, Inscribe Ministries,
Co-Author *The Yielding*

· · · · · · · · · ·

As I read this amazing book about God's angels at work among us, I personally sensed the presence of the Holy Spirit and his angels around me. As we are lifted up in the Lord's presence we can expect to be changed more into His image. Within the pages of this book is fresh encouragement for pressing into His kingdom that is coming among us; there is a call to further increase your hunger and thirst for more of the life of God. "On earth, as it is in heaven."
- Beverly Selby, Prophetic Intercessory Teams Leader,
Westside Vineyard Church, Portland, Oregon

· · · · · · · · · ·

When I first met Bob Blase, it was during my ministry schedule a few years ago at Westside Vineyard Church in Portland, OR. A group of us met in the intercessory prayer room just prior to my ministry time that evening. I was taken completely aback by Bob's depth of seer anointing as he described in intricate details of the visitation of the angels in our prayer room and the messages they conveyed; it was so vivid. I was overwhelmed and intrigued as I learned of the level of angelic encounters that Bob had on a regular basis. You will be swept into an entire, unlimited dimension of God's supernatural realm through Bob's descriptions so that you will find yourself personally hungry for more of this type of kingdom lifestyle. He also offers knowledge that may assist us in getting in touch with these unseen kingdom spheres! Through it all he offers a strong biblical basis, even as he humbly and regularly submits to pastoral accountability.

Notice an example of Bob's angelic experience found in the book, from Chapter 2, "Angel in My Closet": "While I searched my heart for what one might say to a heavenly visitor, the angel spoke first. His words were direct and full of wonder. He said, 'I am here to give you revelation. I am a courier of secrets. The enemy cannot see me. There is a demonic principality operating locally. Assaulting him will be a key.'" After ministering many years in this region, I can certainly attest along with Pastor Arlan Askew that this was an accurate message necessary for multiplication of God's kingdom in this Portland Metro region.

Be prepared to be absolutely amazed, blessed, informed, and instructed as you read and re-read this masterfully documented handbook, written by my seer prophetic brother in the Lord. This book will illuminate your spiritual eyes concerning the value and little-understood purposes of God's heavenly messengers sent forth for the sake of service on our behalf (Hebrews 1:14).

- John Mark Pool, Co-founder of Word to the World Ministries, and Author of *Path of A Prophet* and *Love, God's Greatest Gift*

• • • • • • • • • •

As a pastor for more than forty years I am more than

pleased to see the increased grace and restoration of the equipping ministries of the church. Our call and commission to bring the kingdom of God and push back the gates of hell can only be accomplished by all of the gifts in ministry that the Lord desires for his warrior bride. The apostle Paul explains the diversity and dependency of the body of Christ in I Corinthians 12:14 "for in fact the body is not one member but many," and in the following Scripture he lays out the necessity of all of the spiritual senses to be in operation for the body to operate effectively.

We are so blessed to have the seer prophets in the body of Christ at large and in the local church as well. The activation of this grace allows us to work more closely in synchronization with heaven here on earth. I thank the Lord continually for Bob Blase and the other seer prophets in our local church and the seers across the body of Christ that are being raised up. I believe this book will inspire many to pursue and honor the seer prophets' contributions to the church. In II Kings 6:14-18, the incident of Elijah the seer prophet and his servant gives us assurance the Lord wants to open our eyes so we can see that "there are more for us than against us" and that he is opening our eyes, and blinding the eyes of the enemies of the kingdom of God. As has been said, "The veil is getting thinner between heaven and earth," and our warrior King is at the door!

- Arlan Askew, Senior Pastor, Westside Vineyard Church, Portland, Oregon

. . . .

I know and love the author of *In the Counsel of Angels*,

Bob Blase. I have been very hungry for more understanding, specifically on how the angelic operates. This book has brought an increase to that understanding and has helped me to be more aware of the spiritual realm. Thank you for sharing your life with us Bob, and your intimate experiences with the angels.
- Barbro Askew, Senior Pastor, Westside Vineyard Church, Portland, Oregon

· · · · · · · · · ·

Prepare to have your understanding of the kingdom of God enlarged and challenged as you read this life-transforming book by Bob Blase. The subject of angels is most definitely a controversial subject in the body of Christ today. Bob does a masterful job of not only relating heavenly revelation and insights, but presenting them in balance with Scripture. As you read through the pages of *In the Counsel of Angels*, you will begin to get a glimpse into the spiritual realm that helps bring an anointing for holiness and produces the fear of the Lord. This book has the power of God flowing through its pages; it will stir you deeply and awaken your hunger for deeper intimacy and in your walk with Jesus. Get ready to have a fire lit in you as you become zealous for the Lord and infused with His power to walk in your assignment, bringing heaven to earth.
- Daneen Bottler, Senior Associate Leader, Father's House City Ministries, Portland,Oregon

Psalms 103:20 declares "Bless the LORD, O you his angels, you mighty ones who do his word, obeying the voice of his word!" We are thankful to see God is now raising up a remnant of His people who are committed to obey the Lord's voice and carry out His work. The work of His angels and the work of His church in these last days is merging together to bring about the purpose of God on the earth, so that in the end, Ephesians 1:9-10 would result: "that all things be united in Christ, things in heaven and things on earth."

We are living in a time where God is looking for those He can share His riches and treasures in the heavenly places with, and He has found such a one in our brother, Bob Blase. Bob has been blessed by the Lord and I believe he is called to be a link between the realms of angels and of men. Bob has encouraged and blessed us through the encounters he has shared with us, often helping us to make more sense of our assignments to the city of Portland in intercession and prophetic acts. In Ephesians 3:8 Paul speaks about the unsearchable riches in Christ that is now available to us. This book is not just about angels, it is about the riches of Christ being revealed to His church, which is called to be the fullness of Him that fills all in all.

- Steve Trujillo, Senior Leader, Father's House City Ministries, Portland, Oregon.

IN THE COUNSEL OF ANGELS

THE MINISTRY OF ANGELS
AND MY ASSIGNMENT
FROM JESUS

IN THE COUNSEL OF ANGELS

THE MINISTRY OF ANGELS AND MY ASSIGNMENT FROM JESUS

Bob Blase

IN THE COUNSEL OF ANGELS

Copyright ©2019 Bob Blase. All rights reserved.

No part of this book may be used or reproduced without written permission, except in the case of brief quotations in critical articles and reviews. For more information, contact admin@inscribepress.com

Published by Inscribe Press, Tigard, OR
Cover by Pelton Media Group, Portland, OR

Unless otherwise noted, Bible quotations are taken from the New King James Version. Copyright ©1983 by Thomas Nelson, Inc.
Used by permission. All rights reserved.

Verses marked ESV are from The ESV® Bible (The Holy Bible, English Standard Version®), copyright © 2001 by Crossway, a publishing ministry of Good News Publishers. Used by permission. All rights reserved.

Verses marked BSB taken from The Holy Bible, Berean Study Bible, Copyright ©2016, 2018 by Bible Hub
Used by permission. All rights reserved worldwide.

Verses marked NAS taken from the New American Standard Bible® (NASB), Copyright © 1960, 1962, 1963, 1968, 1971, 1972, 1973, 1975, 1977, 1995 by The Lockman Foundation.
Used by permission. www.Lockman.org

ISBN 978-1-951611-05-7 (Print)
978-1-951611-06-4 (Ebook)

TABLE OF CONTENTS

FOREWORD	15
PREFACE	
Angel in my closet	19
INTRODUCTION	25

CHAPTER 1 CONTACT FROM HEAVEN

Come forth as gold	34
Talk to them	41
Take on His interests	43
Chariot ride to Jesus	45
By revelation of Jesus Christ	48

CHAPTER 2 IN THE COUNSEL OF ANGELS

The counsel of angels	56
Messenger (Lead) angel	58
Destiny angel	62
Battalion Commanders	64
Hawk angel	70
Commander of armies	74
Lion Angel General	78
Angels of Mercy	83
Our sweet Lord Jesus	88

CHAPTER 3 ANGELS AND INTERCESSORS: ALIGNING IN WAR

Ministering spirits sent forth to minister	94
Read the thrones	97
Troop deployment operations	99
Regional angelic activity: to free a region	104
Taking down a satanic prince	107
The three thrones of Portland	110
National angelic activity	121
Under cover of darkness	
Down comes a mountain	124
To the nations: war in the heavenlies over Thailand	128
A mighty cherub on his throne	132

CHAPTER 4 DEMYSTIFYING THE SPIRIT REALM

The unseen is the eternal	140
Dominion is the children's bread	144
Unity and fellowship of the spirit	143
Rebuked by an angel	157

CHAPTER 5 HE IS AT THE DOOR

Become my intercessor	170
Come to the quiet	172
The secret place of abiding	179

I delight to do your will	**183**
The all-access pass	**187**
Tongues of men, tongues of angels	**193**

CHAPTER 6 ANGELS AND MEN: ALIGNING WITH THE WILL OF GOD

The Lord and His hosts	**202**
Revelations and mysteries	**208**
The will of God	**212**
Test the spirits before	**220**
Discernment: seeing through to what is hidden	**225**
Eat your prophecies	**228**
New tongues for new realms	**230**

CHAPTER 7 SNAPSHOTS FROM THE UNSEEN

Heavenly eyes and ears	**238**
Army in my prayer closet	**240**
Pushed by an angel	**242**
My pastors and the spirit realm	**246**
Heavenly anointing of a prophet's words	**249**
Angels' Wings	**250**
Turn aside and see?	**253**

AFTERWORD **255**

ABOUT THE AUTHOR **257**

ARTWORK **259**

FOREWORD

One of the responsibilities of being a pastor includes testing and screening the source and spirit of a matter being released by people. This is a job we take seriously, and although we recognize no human vessel is perfect, we do our best to make sure that Jesus and his Word are always honored. I feel confident this is the case with Bob and his book. Dreams, visions and angelic visits are common in the Bible and in the experience of believers around the world. What Bob shares here is a beautiful example of how God seems to speak to us and reveal Himself in a way that is unique to each of his children, a way that is both distinct and recognizable. As you read, I believe you will not only enjoy the fascinating perspective God is giving through Bob's experiences, but you will recognize the unmistakable voice of Jesus through one of His servants.

It has been almost five years since Bob's first angelic encounter in one of our Sunday evening renewal meetings, and it happened a few months after the Lord brought Bob and his wife to Westside Vineyard Church. Over these years Bob has proven to be not only very spiritually mature and gifted, but also humble, teachable, a team player, and an asset to the leadership and life of the local church.

The experiences, encounters, and insights that Bob shares in this book are "eye-opening" on several levels. For many readers, as was the case for me, I think the book will be eye-

opening regarding giving a fresh perspective. The first request (if I may call it that) in the model-prayer Jesus taught his disciples is "Your kingdom come, Your will be done on earth, as it is in heaven." When you read this book you get a fresh appreciation for the reality that prayers directed and led by the Holy Spirit are bringing His kingdom—His rule and reign—here on earth in very real, dynamic, and world-changing ways.

Secondly, I believe the book is intended by the Holy Spirit to be eye-opening in the sense that he wants every believer to grow in their ability to "fix our eyes not on what is seen, but on what is unseen." In this book, Bob not only stirs up the "earnest desire" needed to grow in the revelatory gifts, but also shares his own journey, insights, and even painful lessons learned in the process of cultivating his own prophetic intercessory calling and discernment gift.

~Micah Askew, Associate Pastor, Westside Vineyard Church, Portland Oregon.

PREFACE

ANGEL IN MY CLOSET

Suddenly, I was no longer alone.

I had discovered that the dark, quiet, and usually undisturbed privacy of our bedroom closet was a perfect place to pray, and for years I had taken advantage of this location for my morning devotions. This particular morning was no exception and it began like most others.

Until, in an instant, I became aware there was a "presence" next to me: something unearthly, mysterious, other-worldly. The sound of this presence was quieter than silence itself, as if all the background noises of this world were suddenly vacuumed up and removed. All I heard was a crisp, rustling sound, which I now know was an angel folding his wings and settling in to his location.

I could *feel* him next to me as he stood in total silence.

Although I did not want to look, fearful curiousity forced me to open my eyes to see what I could see. Looking up, I saw a silhouette in the form of a man standing over me—a man with wings, that is!

I felt peace settle into my spirit as I realized the Spirit of God was vigorously testifying that this angel was one of His, but my flesh continued with its own set of reactions. My body instinctively froze; I was a statue. The little hairs

on the back of my neck stood up, and a cold shiver quickly rippled down my spine. I thought, "There is an angel in my closet. What do I do now?"

My mind raced to imagine why he had come. This was not the first time I had seen an angel. In fact, I was just starting to be somewhat comfortable with the ministering angels that I'd been seeing in our services at church. But this personal visit at my home was a completely unexpected turn.

The atmosphere in that closet was alive and charged with faith, like electricity dancing. I searched my heart for what one might say to a heavenly visitor, but the angel spoke first. His words were direct and full of wonder.

"I am here to give you revelation. I am a courier of secrets. The enemy cannot see me. There is a demonic principality operating locally. Assaulting him will be a key."

Then, just as quickly as he had arrived, he disappeared. I was alone, stunned and amazed. I did not know how to even begin to process such an experience. I even wondered, "Did that actually just happen?" I did jot down his words and later shared the experience with my pastors, mostly for my own spiritual safety.

In Luke 1 we see the story of Mary being visited by the angel Gabriel. The angel announces his message, "Mary, the virgin, will bear the holy Son of God, and name Him Jesus." Her faith-filled response stands in Scripture as a shining example of how to respond to God or His messenger, and His revealed will:

> And Mary said, "Behold, the bond-slave of the Lord; may it be done to me according to your word." And the

angel departed from her. Luke 1:38, NAS.

Thankfully, like Mary, I chose to believe the angel's words and receive God's promises.

Three days later, again while I was in prayer, the same angel returned. Immediately he began to speak.

"It is the Father's good pleasure to give you the kingdom. You will be shown the foundation stones of unbelief in this world and in the spiritual world. You will assault unbelief and strike it with the Word of God. Your words of faith will strike these stones and we will carry out the attacks. Idols will fall. You will work with many of us. Narrow your focus. Narrow your activities. Remember Gideon, and be filled with assurance. For God has chosen you even before you think you are ready. Your own life is finished. You belong to the Risen Christ, who lives and reigns forever." As soon as he finished these words he vanished. Again I was stunned. Though the angel was gone, his words lit up the atmosphere with a vibrancy of life. Joy and holy fear from the Spirit of God poured over my head like water, flooding my whole being, making me aware of the immediacy of God—that He is indeed the "living" God, and that He was looking at and speaking His message to me in real-time.

Some months later it was revealed to me that a portal to heaven had been opened over me. I also learned that this angel was assigned to me as my Lead Angel. Many angels have since presented themselves, along with their assignments, and in some cases, their armies.

Over time and through many changes, I have grown accustomed to expecting things of this nature happening to me.

Well, mostly!

INTRODUCTION

I asked, "What are these, my lord?" The angel who was talking with me answered, "I will show you what they are." Zechariah 1:9, NIV.

God is personal. He is a lover. God loves engaging in relationship with us as we go about doing His will.

Angels are real. The following stories relate some of my first-hand experiences with these messengers sent by God to further His purposes in the earth.

This ministry from the Lord is fully interwoven with my spiritual growth and an increase in knowledge and experience of intimacy with our Lord, of the knowledge of His will, and of learning to recognize and walk in the works He prepared beforehand. And for the body of Christ, this is an affirmation of the value and potency of your intercessory prayers, because through them the power of God is released to effect change in this temporal world we live in. Throughout the book, we will look at some of the ways He has revealed His working in the unseen realm.

Now this is the confidence that we have in Him, that if we ask anything according to His will, He hears us.

> And if we know that He hears us, whatever we ask, we know that we have the petitions that we have asked of Him. 1 John 5:14-15, NKJ.

An angel of the Lord first appeared to me several years ago and began to instruct me about my new assignment from the Lord Jesus. He said, "You will be shown the foundation stones of unbelief in this world and in the spiritual world. You will assault unbelief and strike it with the Word of God. Your words of faith will strike these stones and we will carry out the attacks. Idols will fall. You will work with many of us."

In the Counsel of Angels offers a glimpse of this new assignment from the Lord as it has unfolded to me. You will read of the exchanges the Holy Spirit orchestrates between His holy angels and me. Over the years I have been aware of angelic influence and intervention in my life and in the lives of others. And I have read of, and heard about, people encountering God's holy angels. I am aware of the many accounts recorded in the Bible where angels visited people and ministered to them according to the will of God. Still, the extent of interaction with angels that I describe in these pages was previously unknown to me on an experiential level until just a few years ago. My understanding continues to grow about how the Holy Spirit prepared me for this assignment, though as you will see, angels coming to me at first was completely unexpected.

God's angels began showing up unannounced, as so often is their way. It was a shock to my entire being. It has been an arresting of my attention, a test of my discernment, and a test of my obedience to the Lord. This testing has especially been an on-going test of faith; for all things from God must be

IN THE COUNSEL OF ANGELS

partnered with faith in order to be received. I have recorded in my journal many of the things I have seen and heard while being with the angels. I am sharing a sampling of these things with you, His church and His bride, because the Lord Jesus directed me to do so.

Included with this assignment has come an enhancement of intimacy and friendship with God that is the core pleasure of my life. It is an honor and privilege to share these experiences with you, and the heavenly wisdom, insight, and prophetic releases from God's messengers. Messages from God's angels in no way contradict God's written Word, the Bible. Angelic messengers are employed by the Holy Spirit, and are part of His ministry promised by the Lord Jesus in John 16:13,

> But when He, the Spirit of truth, shall come, He will guide you into all the truth. For He will not speak from Himself, but whatever He may hear, He will speak. And He will declare to you the things coming.

Likewise, the angels of God do not speak or act for themselves, but only according to what God has authorized.

For my part, I have believed in the Lord Jesus Christ for more than forty-five years. God is three-in-one: Father, Son, and Holy Spirit. I am not a Bible scholar, but I am, and continue to be, an enthusiastic student of His holy Word, the Bible. I believe the Bible to be the Holy Spirit-inspired, infallible, eternal Word of God.

> "Heaven and earth shall pass away, but My words shall not pass away." Matthew 24:35.

I have operated in the prophetic ministry of the Holy

Spirit for many decades. It has been of the utmost importance to me to test—by Scripture and by the Holy Spirit—these encounters with angels and to verify their authenticity. When these visitations began I immediately conferred with my pastors, who are my spiritual overseers and my counselors. Together we have biblically and carefully evaluated the nature of my experiences with the angels, and the content of the messages they bring.

Each visitation from an angel has been more than just a conversation or an event. My contacts with the heavenly hosts have brought great enlargement to my awareness of the reality and vastness of the invisible, spirit realm. The power I have experienced from the presence of God's holy angels and from the penetrating nature of their anointed words has regularly pierced me to the depths of heart and soul, and tested me. One angel declared to me, "Do you expect to stand this close to our fire and not be examined and purified by it?"

> And of the angels He says, who makes His angels winds, and His ministers a flame of fire, Hebrews 1:7, NAS.

God made His angels' nature to be flames of fire, for in His nature He is a consuming fire. And

> Therefore, since we receive a kingdom which cannot be shaken, let us show gratitude, by which we may offer to God an acceptable service with reverence and awe; for our God is a consuming fire. Hebrews 12: 28-29, NAS.

In this Kingdom Age, all things in the heavens and the earth are being moved by God toward summation under the rule and reign of Jesus Christ, the resurrected Lord of All. God

IN THE COUNSEL OF ANGELS

is now bringing His kingdom to earth under the banner of His kingdom-purpose, embodied in Jesus' prayer:

> "Your kingdom come. Your will be done, on earth as it is in heaven." Matthew 6:10, NAS.

God's heavenly ministers, His holy angels, are at work here and now and working among us according to this purpose of bringing His kingdom and His will to planet Earth. Many of you already believe and know that His angels are here, and increasingly many individuals are seeing into their workings.

By the grace and calling of God, the Lord has purposed that His angels come and work with me according to His will. This ministry of angels is directly tied to my work and calling as one of His intercessors and as a seer prophet to the body of Christ. Sometimes I simply listen to the message the angels bring. Sometimes we talk together. Other times I watch what the angels are doing. And there are times when Holy Spirit takes me into the spirit realm to go on operations with His angels. Often what the angels say is expressed as being to me personally. Yet, it is clear that often the interpretation of their messages carries a double-meaning of being for the body as well.

When the angels engage with me they come with full awareness of who I am and of my assignment from Jesus (the angels refer to this as my rank). Many of these angels I have come to work with regularly, and I know them by name. However, I have chosen to not mention their names in this book, so that it might not become a distraction. Revealing their names here is not essential to the telling of my story, and the angels don't care. Their concern is always the message and the mission on which God has sent them; it is never about them. This is also a good understanding for us to have towards the ministry of angels; their coming is about the message and the mission they have received from the Lord of hosts. They are sent here to help, assist, enable, or otherwise minister to us with heavenly resources on the Lord's behalf.

> Are they not all ministering spirits, sent out to render service for the sake of those who will inherit salvation?
> Hebrews 1:14, NASB.

A very special thanks to my pastors (who my Lead Angel refers to as "your brothers"), Arlan Askew, Micah Askew, and Paul Pauley, whose grace, spiritual wisdom, and friendship have been a solid source of profound encouragement, and a true calling-forth of what the Lord is doing in my life for the sake of His Body. It is my hope these things I share will encourage you and uplift your faith in the Lord and in His watchful, loving care over you. May your knowledge of His kingdom-workings be expanded and challenged. I thank God for sending to us the help of His mighty heavenly hosts, His angel armies. Do not be afraid, for the Lord of Hosts is with us! Now please turn the pages and read as I report to you God's workings while *In the Counsel of Angels*.

~Bob Blase

CONTACT FROM HEAVEN

COME FORTH AS GOLD

> And Job said, "Look, I go forward, but He is not there, and backward, but I cannot perceive Him; when He works on the left hand, I cannot behold Him; when He turns to the right hand, I cannot see Him. But He knows the way that I take; when He has tested me, I shall come forth as gold. My foot has held fast to His steps; I have kept His way and not turned aside. I have not departed from the commandment of His lips; I have treasured the words of His mouth more than my necessary food." Job 23:8-12, NKJ.

My wife Karen and I were enduring the longest, darkest, most difficult season of trials in our lives when we attended our first Sunday evening service at Westside Vineyard Church, Portland, Oregon in October 2014. We already took part in one of their mid-week home groups, and the Lord's love and comfort through His body was effectively ministering strength and restoration to us.

I was experiencing excruciating chronic body pain and cognitive loss resulting from injuries I received from a high-speed motor vehicle crash fourteen years earlier.

Karen wore a colorful scarf on her hairless head since she had just completed many rounds of chemotherapy and

IN THE COUNSEL OF ANGELS

surgery to remove uterine cancer.

Life's troubles had attacked and battered us, delivering blow after crushing blow. I believe our faith in God survived through the grace of God alone. The many years of being His followers had worked into us the faith to believe He was still working in our lives; but the testing that was upon my wife and me was so severe and so long-standing that our circumstances were relentlessly screaming that God was out of reach.

I somehow still hoped deep inside that He would reappear.

What a beautiful thing it was that Sunday evening to gather with God's people and experience the heavenly worship, the presence of God, the Word preached under a powerful anointing, and a moving time of ministry and prayer afterward. We did not yet know that God was about to lead us out of our dark season. He did not pre-announce His plan. I never saw Him approaching. He never explained that He was about to open a new chapter in our lives; He just did it. (Months later, hindsight helped me see that He had prepared my heart and I was ready for anything He had for us.)

A prayer line had formed after the preaching. The visiting ministers, Mathai and Mariyamma Mathai, Apostles to India and friends of our pastors, began to pray for each person in the line. I was sensing the presence of the Spirit of God intensifying around us, and upon me, as they worked their way down the prayer line. They got to me and I suppose they both quickly saw how broken and needy I was. As they gently placed their hands on me it felt as though time stopped. Mariyamma prayed a simple, but powerfully personal prophetic prayer over me; just six words: "Show him Your will, my Master. Show him Your will, my Master." Mathai stood by my side, embracing me with compassion, humility, and gentleness that only comes from knowing the Lord Jesus Christ intimately. The Lord's comfort was so real. It was as if Jesus was there, saying through these ministers' actions, "I've got you. I understand. I never left you." Mariyamma repeated those words of her prayer slowly, maybe five or six times. The Spirit was testifying in my spirit that it was His appointed time for me. He was about to cause a spiritual shift in my life, in our lives; a new setting of my course; an alignment of my life with Him and His will and purposes. Deep inside I whispered, "Lord, let me be ready. Let it be so."

God approached me so softly and gently that night. No fireworks, no sparks, or heavenly jolts of power, but simply a powerful and peaceful assurance of faith in His faithfulness. While on a personal level I was a man undone, by God's gift I was also yielded to Him. It was a few years later when Holy Spirit caused me to see that the ministers and I had been ushered right then into a glory encounter, one of impartation and transformation. The new thing He did was profound beyond my human imagination. He touched me in my spirit man and my human soul at a depth that only God Himself can access. He internally reset the course of my life at a pivot point from which He radically elevated the trajectory of how I know Him and how I see His kingdom.

Through our long season of trials my wife and I had placed our trust in the Lord, and our faith in God seemed to be the only evidence of hope during those years of indescribable pressures. If our trials were a crucifixion and death with Christ, then this resetting was certainly a resurrection with Christ and a revealing of His life and glory. As the apostle Paul wrote,

> "I have been crucified with Christ; it is no longer I who live, but Christ lives in me; and the life which I now live in the flesh I live by faith in the Son of God, who loved me and gave Himself for me." Galatians 2:20, NKJ.

Over time, the Spirit has opened up whole new dimensions of how my wife and I experience the Lord's love, our closeness to Him and His will, and the fellowship of the Spirit with members of the Body. The events in this book testify to the fruit of God's working.

God is still in the business of appointing times and seasons in the lives of men. This is true for us all, paupers, kings, and those in-between. His wisdom, might, knowledge, and light are the impartations during these appointed times and seasons; for the Lord is a lavish giver. He still reveals His deep and secret plans to the hearts of men. God moved to freshly align me with Himself; with His will and the assignment He had purposed to reveal to me.

> Behold, I will do something new. Now it will spring forth; will you not be aware of it? I will even make a roadway in the wilderness, rivers in the desert.
> Isaiah 43:19, NASB.

"A roadway in the wilderness," and "rivers in the desert" as mentioned in the Bible would be two things that are thought of as altogether impossible. It is as if God is saying in this verse, "I will do something new. It will be so impossible that you will know that I, and only I, am the One doing it." God can show His favor, even to what was the inhospitable and uninhabitable wasteland of our lives. Oh, the arrogance of our human misery, to suggest that anything could prevent Almighty God from intervening and participating in our lives! Even when you are convinced that God has forgotten you and He can no longer reach you; that is, in fact, completely untrue. I know, because I was there in my life. Yes, He will do the impossible. Now, it will spring up. Will you again have faith? Are you ready for it? He asks us, "Will you be aware of it?" The verse implies it is possible for God to initiate something new in our life, and we might not even our notice it. It is of great benefit to live with an expectancy of good from Him; to trust in His goodness and faithfulness. Will you notice when His new thing comes? Will you believe it?

I have wondered how many burning bushes Moses walked past before he "turned aside to see" and discovered the angel waiting for him. God loves us so much that He wants to bless us and be with us. He wants our attention so we can know He is giving us His attention. He is a relational God, an interactive heavenly Father who loves His children. When He works in your life it is His goal to have your participation in an ever-growing, ever-increasing way. Sometimes our lives are too filled with other things to give God the attention that He deserves and requires. The Father wants to give all His love to our souls. Is it too much for Him to ask for the attention of our souls that we might receive all He has for us?

There is a purpose to God's wilderness; it is a place of preparation. The wilderness can be like a birth canal to deliver the emergence of the promises of God in our lives. In the narrow and constricting way of the wilderness I was poised to learn the lesson of a lifetime. This lesson from God would not so much teach me as it would transform me. It would reset my

IN THE COUNSEL OF ANGELS

paradigm from living my life with a self-oriented perspective, to experiencing life through a Christ-oriented perspective. To simply know this with my mind would not have changed me. There had to be a meeting of my heart with God. It seems this had to be learned through hunger, testing, and humbling. As I recall, there are many stories in the Bible that attest to God dealing with folks similarly. The ways of man will fail us, but those who place their trust in Him will not be disappointed.

Persevere through the test. If you obey God in the wilderness, agreeing to do His will, He will bring you into the land of His promise. I would not trade this lesson for anything in this world. According to His promise, He has built a highway through my uninhabitable land and has set a flowing stream through my desert wasteland. This is access to the "life more abundantly" which Jesus promised us.

How great is our God!

> IF YOU OBEY GOD IN THE WILDERNESS, AGREEING TO DO HIS WILL, HE WILL BRING YOU INTO THE LAND OF HIS PROMISE.

> Therefore, do not throw away your confidence, which has a great reward. For you have need of endurance, so that when you have done the will of God, you may receive what was promised.
> Hebrews 10:35-36, NAS.

He really does take us all onward and upward as we continue to trust Him. He takes us from grace to grace, faith to faith, strength to strength, and glory to glory.

> Now to Him who is able to do far more abundantly

beyond all that we ask or think, according to the power that works within us; to Him be the glory in the church and in Christ Jesus to all generations forever and ever. Amen. Ephesians 3:20-21, NAS.

TALK TO THEM

For God is the One working in you both to will and to work according to His good pleasure. Philippians 2:13.

Over a period of months, I was being mightily impacted by the power of God, particularly during ministry times at church through the ministry team's prayers and the laying on of hands. I received much spiritual encouragement and physical healing, including relief from severe chronic pain. I had sustained injuries to my spine and head from the high-speed motor vehicle crash many years earlier. As team members would pray for people, I began to see that angels also were placing their hands on the people.

As time passed, I learned to ask the Holy Spirit for His advice on how to respond to His angels. At one point He suggested I talk to them. That made sense, but it was also a bit unnerving. The first time I spoke to an angel was a time when again people were praying for me. I was laid out on the floor and experiencing the power of God moving on me. If you had been there looking on, you would have seen me writhing and groaning, but inwardly I was experiencing a heavenly peace. I saw in the spirit that I lay there in perfect stillness. Six angels were kneeling around me and ministering to me with their hands. Soon, I could no longer see the people that were around me, but only the angels. The angel nearest my face had his arm all the way past his elbow reaching inside my chest. I asked him a question, and to my amazement, he answered me.

"What are you doing?" I said.

He answered, "I am rewiring your spine." I was literally shocked speechless. This angel had answered me. We were in contact, face to face. Had they crossed into our natural realm to appear and speak with me? Or, had I crossed into the spirit realm? In the days that followed, I kicked myself a few times for not asking the angel some follow-up questions. But I was just learning how to communicate with them, and I certainly did not realize then that there would be many more opportunities ahead to interact with them.

Angelic encounters during these ministry times continued over the months, and the Lord also kept imparting more healing and relief from chronic pain, bulging discs, head injury, and PTSD. Praise His Name! The healing of the Lord I received through the prayers of the saints and the ministering spirits was amazing and wonderful. But there was no way I could have known that it was as an introduction to a heavenly assignment He had prepared in advance for me and that was soon to be revealed.

TAKE ON HIS INTERESTS

For as many as are led by the Spirit of God, these are sons of God. Romans 8:14.

The cry of my heart had become, "God, show me what is next for me." When we pray to God we believe He hears us, and that He will answer. Sometimes His answers will show up as a big surprise! Although I already partly understood my calling to prayer, the following encounter came as one of the earliest visitations and had a powerful impact on me.

On a certain day, I entered my prayer closet, greeted God, and prayed the Lord's Prayer from the heart. I was asking the Lord to make those words become my true ultimate desire. My praying in English changed to tongues. It was a tongue I had never heard before. I felt to stand. I could tell the Holy Spirit was pulling me into the glory realm. Then my spirit cried out with groaning and gut-felt bellowing; I almost doubled over. (Yes, my reaction—my outburst—surprised me at the time.) My skin began to crawl, similar to a fear-response, though my heart was at peace. I realized that someone was approaching; someone impressive, someone supernatural. Just then, two feet from me appeared a great angelic brown bear. Next to him was my Lead Angel. This huge bear had massive black wings and his giant face was almost up against mine. He spoke in an angelic language that sounded like the roaring of a bear, wagging his head and showing his teeth as he spoke.

My Lead Angel had already instructed my spirit how to interpret the angel languages into English. I stood looking at him, literally shaking. I had to hold on to a coat rack bar in the closet to steady myself.

The Bear Angel said, "I am the jealousy of God. Like a bear when robbed of her cubs who then meets a man, the Lord your God is a jealous God. He will fight for those who are His. He will give Himself for the battle. Who will fight like Him? Who will fight as passionately as He does? You are to take on His interests; to do His bidding. Your path is fixed. You will be accelerated now. But, you will also remain in your position. Continue to be mindful of the safety we have highlighted to you; that of walking in submission and humility. Do not be alarmed by the things you will be shown, but know that God is at perfect peace. You will not step off the path and become driven by the things you see. You will only follow the Spirit."

The two angels then quickly vanished, though I was still aware of Holy Spirit's watchful care. I was arrested and frozen in place, suspended in a heavenly dimension. I stood motionless and I felt my strength leave me. I exhaled and nearly collapsed to the floor. The power of the angel's message, combined with the fear and holiness of God the angel released on me, impacted me profoundly.

CHARIOT RIDE TO JESUS

The Son is the radiance of God's glory and the exact representation of His nature, upholding all things by His powerful word. Hebrews 1:3a, BSB.

I was in prayer and had been interacting with an angel when instantly, I was in another place and all alone. I was suspended in thin air and surrounded by blue skies, up, down, and all around. Soon, in the distance I saw a flaming horse approaching. The horse was running through the air and pulling a chariot driven by a single angel. They were all covered in orange flames of fire; the horse, the chariot, and the angel. I stared in amazement, watching as they drew near. They pulled up alongside of me and stopped, but the angel said nothing. I stood there for a moment and hesitated, realizing what was about to happen to me. I went ahead and climbed into the chariot, also stepping into the flames of fire. I sensed no heat associated with the fire. What I did sense was holiness, truth, the fear of the Lord, and the vibrancy of the Spirit of Life Himself. The angel and I did not speak to one another as I sat down on a bench inside the chariot, and we were off. Up through the sky we went, moving into a vast expanse of darkened heavens.

We emerged from the darkened skies into the light of a rich, blue sky dotted with beautiful, puffy, white clouds. The flames disappeared from my ride. The horse, the angel, and

the chariot were all then a pure white. In the far distance I saw a light descending, bright as a star. It landed on some of the distant clouds with an explosion of light and power that radiated outwards like a massive shockwave. The light itself then took on the form of a man clothed in light, who appeared to be about fifty feet tall. As we got closer to the Light Man his size was getting smaller. This was odd to me, because on earth when you get closer to an object it gets larger.

We stopped just in front of the Light Man, who now seemed to be a bit over six feet tall. I knew then that I was about to meet the Risen Christ. I climbed down out of the chariot. As I approached Jesus, He put out His arms to welcome me. We embraced and He kissed my neck and forehead. He did not let me out of His embrace, and His Presence was so weighty, so full of warmth and truth and glory. I can only attempt to describe what He was like.

Jesus really is made of love. His love surrounded me with the sense of the worth and value that He has for me. And, He is the most humble and genuine person I have ever met. Living Scriptures were swirling around Him. The ones I could read spoke of His love and declared that He is the Word of God and the image of God. I knew these qualities describe the very heart of the Living God, Creator of all things, Love Eternal.

Spirit-to-spirit he spoke with me, saying, "Everything We do is because of Our love for you" ("you" referred to every person in the human race). He said He brought me to that place to reinforce in me that He loved me, and He wanted His love to be the reason I did the things He has for me. He knew I was wondering why we did not meet in heaven itself. He said, "I wanted us to meet alone this time so there would be no distractions." After Jesus left, I still felt suspended in this heavenly dimension. The Spirit reminded me of the provision Christ made for us all, to abide in Him through the power of the Holy Spirit (see John 14: 17, and 15: 4-10).

BY REVELATION OF JESUS CHRIST

> Paul, an apostle sent not from men nor by man, but by Jesus Christ and God the Father, who raised Him from the dead. For I certify to you, brothers, that the gospel I preached is not devised by man. I did not receive it from any man, nor was I taught it; rather, I received it by revelation from Jesus Christ,
> Galatians 1:1, 11-12, BSB.

If you want to know why Jesus chose to interact this way with me, I can tell you what He said when I asked Him that very question. He answered me, "I am doing this with you this way because I want to."

For me, that was enough. I said simply, "Yes Lord."

Part of my Lead Angel's charge is to familiarize me with my assignment from the Lord, keep me focused, and escort me through it. One day the angel explained to me, "Your assignment to intercession was so you could find Him in the secret place; and to learn of Him and take on His interests. Delighting to do His will opened the door to the heavenly assignment with all of us, for we always do His will. We told you we would take you on a tour of the expanse of your assignment and that your kingdom authority increases at the same time. Remember the Joshua 1:3 kingdom key; every place your foot treads is given to you. Share this with others who are taking ground. Do not succumb to the temptation to want to see evidence in the natural realm to validate your faith. You are fighting the good fight that is by faith. Let all the kingdom warriors raise their voices and shout. What about being so attuned in your spirit and in your heart that you are always prepared to listen to Him? Remember the gold-standard we are aiming for, where Jesus said 'I only do what I see the Father doing,' and 'greater works shall you do.'

"Are those markers too hard to hit; too far away? I think not. They are markers that a son and a daughter are to aim for. This is on the path of abiding in Him by faith; that is where the greater works will present themselves. These things are yours now for a possession and an ownership. They are to increase in the body unto the fullness of the stature of Christ. Remember, take heed how you hear!"

On another occasion Jesus said, "I want you to stay at your assignment. I am using you to help push the envelope on this one. I want the nature of the work of My (Angel) Armies revealed. Take what you have received and leaven the whole lump."

He was referring to the revelations and wisdom that His angels bring to me, and how He wants me to take what I have received and give it out to His body, the church. I never consciously asked for, or prayed for this, nor did it ever enter my imagination that God would have me working with His angels. I do not consider myself an authority on the angelic or the spirit realm. Almighty God, the Creator of all things, and His unseen kingdom are just too unimaginably big. He spans infinity and eternity! It is enough for me to receive His love as His son, and to seek to be a faithful follower of His by being obedient to His Word and to the heavenly vision.

In the Scripture quoted at this beginning of this section, Paul states he received his mission and even his message directly from the Lord, and not from men. He did not get his message from another preacher's sermon, from Bible college or seminary, off a CD, from YouTube, or from any other action of man. He said, "I received it by revelation from Jesus Christ." In similar fashion, the revelations I am sharing with you in this book were not devised by man. I did not receive them from any man, nor was I taught them; but I received them by revelation of Jesus Christ, and from His angels. I am certainly not the first person to receive an assignment directly from Jesus, nor am I the last. Let's be clear: I am in no way even remotely comparing myself to Paul. What I am saying is that I too got my message and this assignment from above, by revelation from Jesus Christ, and not from anyone on the earth. Prior to Jesus talking directly with me about these things, He was pleased to send His heavenly messengers to me to activate this assignment.

> TO BE IN JESUS' PRESENCE IS TO BE WITH LOVE ETERNAL, AND TO NEVER WANT TO LEAVE HIM. HIS LOVE FOR US IS FILLED WITH A PASSION BEYOND WORDS

The call precedes the commissioning. I heard the call to serve Him fully many decades ago, and received many confirmations and consecrations along the way. Even as a young boy I sensed I would somehow give my life wholly in service to God, though I had no idea at the time what that meant—nor did I have that sense at a conscious level—so I could not even articulate it. Really, God's preparation process for this assignment has spanned my entire lifetime, and that includes many times of crushing and humbling of self. From my perspective it often looks like a meandering trail of "trials and errors"; countless trials and endless errors! It has been a conscious walk of faith in Him for over forty-five years—through much prayer, study, worship, work, hardship, travail, repentance, giving, forgiveness, listening, waiting, learning, serving, blessing, testing, suffering, distraction, failing, questioning, proving, pruning, rejoicing, shaping, molding, surrender, and blessing. Through it all, God remains God. He called me using the words He had Jeremiah record,

> See, I have appointed you this day over the nations and over the kingdoms, to pluck up and to break down, to destroy and to overthrow, to build and to plant."
> Jeremiah 1:10.

Walking in the will of God has come as a progressive revelation through the acceptance by faith of His undeserved grace, and by taking on His interests and abandoning my own agendas. It remains a constant challenge of walking in faith and trust, apart from my own carnal reasoning and the influences of earth-bound opinions from carnally minded men. This combines with the Holy Spirit's assignment to me as one of His intercessors. Don't you love how walking in the Spirit in obedience to Jesus engages with Him, where He shares with us intimate concerns and priorities that are on His heart?

To be in Jesus' presence is to be with Love eternal, and to never want to leave Him. His love for us is filled with a passion beyond words, just like the Scriptures reveal: "For God so loved the world that He gave His only begotten Son…"; "Behold

what manner of love the Father has bestowed upon us that we should be called sons of God…"; and "As the Father has loved Me, so have I loved you." He is truly irresistible!

These realities motivate me to love, serve, and obey Him. I pray that by His grace you will seek to always abide in Him, walk in His revelation light, and serve Him with humility, holiness, and unflinching obedience.

> Speaking the truth in love, may grow up into him in all things, which is the head, even Christ. Ephesians 4:15.

This is His call. It is our destiny!

IN THE COUNSEL OF ANGELS

THE COUNSEL OF ANGELS

Then I said, "What are these, my lord?" The angel who talked with me said to me, "I will show you what they are." Zechariah 1:9, ESV.

God places angels all around us. Some angels actually encamp—abide—around us. Many believers are becoming more aware of the presence of these assigned angels. When we are not in immediate need of being delivered, what else do you suppose these abiding angels do? Holy Spirit has many of His angels working with Him to be our enablers, to help in our callings and assignments from the Lord. The Holy Spirit did not give me advance notice that He was going to set up a group of angels to encamp around me as counselors. He just assigned them, and had me learn as I moved forward in obedience. (I am still learning, incidentally.) It is the kingdom way: the learning is in the doing, and the doing is by faith.

Since the angels appointed to me have come as counselors, I decided to refer to them as the Council of Angels. I am talking about eight angels who stand in a circle, which includes me and one of the angels sharing the six o'clock position. The angels always stand, while I am most often comfortably seated. These angels have come to help me and

IN THE COUNSEL OF ANGELS

advise me of God's plans. They equip me in how to work with them in ongoing and upcoming angelic operations.

They introduced themselves to me one by one, for the most part, over the span of a couple of years. Each new angel to appear and abide took up a position in the circle, beginning at six o'clock and then proceeding counterclockwise. By the time five angels had filled a half-circle, I surmised the circle would likely be complete when the number was eight.

Angels are true ambassadors of the kingdom of heaven. They would be the first to tell you that all the glory and power belongs to God. Each of these angels radiates with glory and kingdom authority. You can feel it in their presence, watch it in their demeanor, and hear it when they speak. Often, the glory and power of God that radiates from them melts away my strength. Fortunately they, and Holy Spirit, are capable of toning it down, just so my flesh can handle being in their presence! At times, they will even impart strength back into me by the same Spirit who raised Christ from the dead.

> OFTEN, THE GLORY AND POWER OF GOD THAT RADIATES FROM THE ANGELS MELTS AWAY MY STRENGTH.

I have given names to the types of angels mostly in an effort to describe them for their attributes and assignments. It is not my intention to appear dogmatic about the different types of angels. All of us have so much we can learn about the heavenly things. Though I will not mention their proper names, I have included the general meanings of their names within my descriptions.

MESSENGER (LEAD) ANGEL

This Messenger Angel is my Lead angel. He is a strategist, an idol-smasher, and so much more. Part of our mission together is to assault spiritual strongholds and idolatry as the Spirit directs. He also has scrolls that are the master blueprints of God's intents for cities and nations. This angel was the first angel to appear and speak to me while I was by myself. He is the "angel in my closet" encounter. He is the ranking officer and Chief Counselor among my Council of Angels. The Lord has appointed him as the angelic overseer of my training and the steward of my assignment with the Holy Spirit. Although I call him by name, in this book he is referred to as my Lead Angel.

I respect and honor this angel whom Jesus has assigned to me. And the angels do command respect. They are heavenly and majestic; however, I do not worship this angel. If I were to try for some weird reason, I can guarantee you he would put a stop to it with "the quickness":

> And I am John, who heard and saw these things. And when I had heard and seen them, I fell down to worship at the feet of the angel who had shown me these things. But he said to me, "Do not do that! I am a fellow servant with you and your brothers the prophets, and with those who keep the words of this book. Worship God!"
> Revelation 22:8-9.

IN THE COUNSEL OF ANGELS

Every angel of God and every holy heavenly being shares this same mindset.

Here is a more detailed description of this angel. He appears man-like in form, but with wings of feathers. He is nearly seven feet tall, and is dressed in a gleaming white, full-length robe that has bright golden embellishments across the torso, as well as around his arms and waist. His shoulder-length hair is also pure white. His skin tone is like amber-colored swirled marble. His eyes are a piercing blue. His voice is strong and clear, and kind. His manner is direct and to the point. He is awesome! On one occasion the Holy Spirit said to me regarding this angel, "There is something you should know about this angel of Mine. There is no situation that can come to you that he cannot handle. He has full information, full knowledge, full wisdom and insight about your life and destiny. We will be surprised at nothing!" (The Spirit said that last sentence with a bit of a chuckle.) "This is what you call complete oversight. To remember this will be invaluable to you as you go forward from faith to faith."

This angel has taught me that to trust in what he says to me is in effect also a form of trusting in the Spirit's leading, because his words to me are from the Holy Spirit, and he is God's messenger delivering the message. I am to obey and trust, for Scripture teaches

> **Trust in the Lord with all your heart, and do not lean on your own understanding. Proverbs 3:5.**

Angels do not replace the Holy Spirit, any more than military troops replace the commander who sent them. Angels augment and implement Holy Spirit's work and ministry. You cannot

imagine the arduous, grueling, incremental process over several years it took me to come to trust God that His angels speak for Him. It went well beyond just caution and discernment. This test plowed me headlong into owning and repenting of my own internalized doubt, skepticism, and unbelief. These conditions in the heart are lethal contaminants to our faith. The Lord has been so faithful, patient, and gracious to continue to nurture my faith and understanding, and to purge doubt and unbelief from my heart and soul. His Word is powerful.

> "Already you are clean (purged) because of the word that I have spoken to you." John 15:3, ESV.

I thank Him for His great patience towards us all. Coming to believe in the heavenly things is essential to our continued growth and development in our spirit man. Can you imagine what Jesus' life and ministry might have been like if He had refused to believe in the heavenly things?

The following exchange with my Lead Angel was among the early encounters I had with him. He had been facing me; then he stopped speaking and turned to the side as if he prepared to leave. I could now see part of his wing, and its feathers. On our previous meeting I had asked him his name, but he did not answer me. Now he stopped and told me his name. Then he explained that he carries the keys of wisdom and knowledge to bring down idolatry. A major stronghold of idolatry to be targeted, he identified as "unbelief."

Another time, I was in prayer, alternating with tongues and thanks. I felt to turn my attention to my Lead Angel, standing to my right. He immediately said to me, "Hold. Hold your position. The flames will not kill you. They cannot kill you.

They will instead make you shine. The more you shine with the Lord's glory, the more effective your life will be for Him. You are being prepared to comprehend the power of the Word of God. With wisdom and discernment you will place the Word of God at the precise point of entry for maximum effect. Do not let the confirmations that come surprise you. See, I have told you. Remember, grace and truth comes by Jesus Christ. When your demeanor and your aim are coordinated with His will, then we can add levels of power-release you have only dreamed about. This also represents an increase in your dependency on the Spirit, and your intimacy with Him. It is the 'you in Him, and He in you.' Now continue to endure hardness as a good soldier of Jesus Christ."

I am so grateful this angel does not leave my side.

DESTINY ANGEL

The Destiny Angel is an abiding angel. Though always present, I rarely hear him speak. He ministers mostly through impartation. There is a large company of these angels that have been assigned to our church. Their encampment is at the property of one of our pastors. When revelation from the Spirit is present regarding our identity in Christ and our destiny in God, I can often sense or see the active impartation from the angels who are part of this company. This Destiny Angel came up from behind me and stationed himself at my back when we visited our associate pastors who live in the country. He began to share his assignment with me. He is from a company of angels I am calling Destiny Angels. These angels carry the spirit of faith and impart it to us. They serve to infuse faith into a person's revelation of their identity in Christ, and their calling and destiny in God. They carry the book (scrolls) of destiny for the person they are assigned to. As an operation of the Holy Spirit, I have at times seen when the Spirit assigns these angels to people. The assigned angel abides with the person and assists the Holy Spirit in leading them in their heavenly identity and God's calling on their life. God is truly passing out angels and assignments.

One of my first encounters with what I refer to as a Destiny Angel happened during the ministry time on a Sunday evening service. I was in a prayer circle with a couple of other guys and we were receiving infilling and fresh encouragement

IN THE COUNSEL OF ANGELS

from the Holy Spirit and giving God glory. Just then an angel manifested nearby in the spirit and walked over towards us. We all spontaneously began to holler, shout, and laugh as the angel drew near. I told my friends an angel full of glory had just walked up to us, and then we all yelled. I felt in the spirit that I was to go and get pastor Paul, who also was close by. I told him an angel had shown up and I was supposed to get him. He called his wife and I led them to where the angel was. The silent language, communication from the angel's spirit to my spirit, was coming off of the angel and I began interpreting for the people around me. I told Paul and Jeanna the angel said he was their angel and was coming home with them. When I said that, they both hollered and went backwards and fell upon the elevated stage. The angel continued to speak so I told them the angel said he was bringing his company with him. They planned to set up camp in the woods on the hill behind their house. Paul got up and told me that because I had never been to their house, I wouldn't know what it was like. He said, "There is a hill behind our house, and there are woods on the hill."

Several weeks later we did go to their property. We went into the woods on the hill behind their house and sure enough, the presence of these angels was there. In fact, the presence of God's angels was very noticeable in several locations on their six acres of land!

BATTALION COMMANDERS

The three Battalion Commanders are from a group they call the Angels of the Eagle's Eye (I will introduce the eagles in a moment). These angels are stewards of God's Word. They follow our faith-filled words (declarations)—watching over His words to perform them. They also assist with intercessory assignments by revealing and prioritizing prayer targets, and by giving strategic wisdom. Then, their troops follow the words to the prayer targets and exert their prescribed influence according to the plans of the Spirit.

Battalion Commander One is a keeper of secrets. His name means "patience," for many of his prayer assignments are connected to long-term strategies. He reveals secret operations of the Spirit and His angels, and what my role in them is to be. Much of what he reveals is largely unmentionable, but is essential for the targeted intercessory work the Spirit involves me in. Intercessors especially will be thankful to have these type angels helping them with revelation insight and wisdom for their very important forerunner work of intercession.

Battalion Commander Two is a guardian of the fruitfulness of the Word. His name means the "fruitful one." He oversees kingdom planting of words and its kingdom fruit. He and his angels serve God by attending to the faith-borne kingdom declarations that go forth from our mouths, overseeing the increase of fruit that will remain. This one is the main spokesman and senior officer present for the three.

Battalion Commander Three is the scholarly one, a master teacher; his name means "body of knowledge." He is full of wisdom and instruction: He gives out detailed explanations of Scriptures, truths, dealings, plans, and operations of the Spirit. Because he speaks from the vantage point of heaven, his instruction is packed with revelation and illumination. He is the angel who has helped to advise me on how to prepare, write, and organize the contents of this book. (If the book is a mess, blame me, not the angel. I'm the one who is humanly flawed.)

This is how the Battalion Commanders arrived. I was in a personal prayer and worship time when my spiritual eyes were opened to see three angels in front of me that I had not seen before. Their visage was strong, radiating power from the presence of the Holy Spirit. Each was dressed in a long, white linen robe. Over that was a red leather tunic, and each one carried a long sword at his side. This presentation gave them a military look. Each angel had a living, celestial Golden Eagle standing with one leg on each of the angel's shoulders, and each eagle's body lay forward upon the angel's head, with eagle wings outstretched to a span of about five feet.

I asked the angels, "What is the nature of your visit?"

The Senior Officer spoke up and said, "We are Battalion Commanders. We command the angels you have sensed above you. You and others have prayed to understand our purposes. We are here to tell you." (The previous day, I told one of our prophetic intercessors that I sensed a large number of angels in the sky above me. At that time, this was another "first" for me. She asked the Lord to reveal them to me and tell why they were there. It is so great to have kingdom-minded prayer partners!)

Though the Holy Spirit was strongly confirming His presence, I decided to go through the formal process of testing their spirits. I interrupted the commander and asked them all, "Has Jesus Christ come in the flesh?" All three angels promptly affirmed. "Jesus Christ has come in the flesh." I also asked, "Did Jesus Christ rise from the dead?" In unison they said, "Jesus Christ rose from the dead." Their manner was at once profoundly regal and authoritative, and yet they were also graciously humble. These are characteristics of God which He placed in them when He created them.

Then, the commander delivered his message, "I can tell you are concerned you might miss something we have for you. Don't be. It is our way to not allow you to miss what we have for you. You only would miss out if you were to rebel. So be at peace. It is the kingdom way. Do not let the enormity of the responsibility throw you off. All things are by God's grace. We will bring organization and structure to your assignment and your resources. We represent three full battalions, 1,500 angels each. You are now mitered into us."

I am familiar with the meaning of a miter joint; still it seemed the angel had something else in mind as well. I looked up the definitions of "miter." He waited as I searched. A "miter" is the name of the hat worn by a bishop that symbolizes his responsibility and authority. It is the angel's way of telling me I am a bishop with them, or overseer. This is a heavenly authority dynamic, not an earthly one; it is a promotion, and one that is undergirded by mutual honor and respect between us in the Spirit. This is a confirmation of what the Lion Angel General (this one will be introduced to you later), my Lead Angel, and the Holy Spirit have said to me regarding the development of

IN THE COUNSEL OF ANGELS

my interactions with the angels.

The commander continued, "You have been separated for service to Him. He is the One putting you in-charge of these things. Now ask yourself this question, 'Where is His kingdom rule to be established?'"

I replied, "In men's hearts."

"Exactly. Over time you will learn our structure. You are still learning our ways. So be patient, take it all in."

On another occasion the same commander spoke to me and said, "The growing and the stretching must continue according to the heavenly vision. Yes, it is a good distance from here to there. But rest assured we will take you there. You cannot ponder or quantify the new growth until it is come. It is part of the new creation, and for you it is something that has not yet been seen. Put your confidence in this, that when the new growth appears it will magnify Christ. For God only builds now according to the new creation, and the blueprint is Christ Jesus. Still, the fire will test everything that is built. For that which results from the will of flesh and the will of man will not survive the fire's test. Many people will boast of many things, but everything is tried by fire. Only what is built on God's sure foundation with the tested materials of gold, silver, and precious stones will survive. The eyes of the Lord really are in every place beholding the good and the evil. You are His watchman. We are Angels of the Eagle's Eye. We are sent to tell you what you need to know, to make you see what you need to see, and to take you where you need to be."

As I pondered the angel's words, I marveled that I was hearing words spoken by a being from heaven. I had faith to believe what the angel has prophesied; faith to reach out and

dream of greater things. As so often is the case with the angels, his words spoken from the heavenly realm call forward my awareness of my new man in Christ—my true identity.

Recently, I took a walk in the evening and spoke in tongues nearly non-stop. The silent language from the angel the next morning told me I was hearing revelation from him that day because I invested in their language the night before.

> (...but in his spirit he speaks mysteries. 1 Cor. 14:2b).

In the Council circle on another occasion, I watched as the celestial eagle atop the angel's shoulders drew his wings back into his sides and stood upright. I have never seen them do this before and it caught my attention. I wondered what the message to me might be. I spoke in tongues as I continued to watch. After a few moments, I heard the angels' silent language ask me, "Have you ever wondered why we have eagles over us? Did you think they were just extravagant ornaments?"

He then continued out loud, "We are all in the Holy Spirit, and so, we are one. And yes, our eagles fly reconnaissance missions for us, and then report back. The Spirit could easily just tell you, or He could tell me and then I tell you. But these are kingdom ways, and for this mission we are sending out our eagles. They are to fly and go look into the lives of those who are in the body. Then they will report back to us what they have seen. We will by revelation give insight and words to the intercessors and the shepherds. These will be timely words that will touch each person's heart uniquely, personally, and intimately to build them up in the new man in Christ. This is one way we do this. You know I am not talking about head knowledge. This is about the life-flow of God and His

IN THE COUNSEL OF ANGELS

purposes in the Church. This will be coming in at a new level for the body. Be in prayer about this, especially praying in the Spirit, as these operations involve the secret motives of men's hearts and the mysteries of the kingdom being revealed. This is a part of ministering in the holy things. This is acceleration, a release of life, and a release of the ministry of the Spirit through you all. The key here remains, 'I delight to do Your will, O God'. Tell everyone it is a great joy for us to help the Father's children. Open your hearts and welcome our help."

The Angel Commander raised his left hand in front of him. A small blue cloud appeared just above him. He said, "Tell the children that the Spirit never stops working with them. He never sleeps. He never takes a break. He never takes a day off. He never tires. He abides with you and in you. Walk with Him. Learn from Him, about His love and care. He will never leave you. Men may disappoint, but He will not abandon you."

HAWK ANGEL

This is a heavenly creature who looks like our earthly hawks, except that his body is perhaps seven feet long. The things in heaven were created before the natural universe. So really, our earthly hawks look very much like these heavenly hawks, though downscaled in size. His name means "the gift," which I believe is a reference to God's grace. He is a precious gift, a spirit of entreaty, who also imparts faith in the Father's faithfulness. He is one of the gentlest spirits I have ever met. He and his hawks carry the gift of mercy. These ministering spirits assist Holy Spirit in His appeals to us by constantly pleading, even begging members of the body to come closer to the Lord—in repentance if needed—and to embrace the process of sanctification in humility; the transformation of our souls. They also eat the dead flesh that believers repent of when they cast their burdens on the Lord. Their ministry is a part of the "cast your cares on Him for He cares for you" operation. This creature's raptor-like eyes flash with higher-order heavenly intelligence and laser-sharp discernment; and of course, he can speak.

Here is how I met this heavenly creature. I felt the Spirit's nudge to go and sit with my Council of Angels. I began to speak in tongues. It was a new tongue. Soon a large Hawk Angel settled in at the 10:30 position in the Council circle. At this time, I had not seen a Hawk Angel of this size. As he entered, his silent language was speaking. It told me his name

IN THE COUNSEL OF ANGELS

and said, "I am one of the Hawk Angels who are with you all. I have seen all around the body. I am a surveyor of the spirits of men, a watchman. When needed, I will give a report on people or on conditions in the spirit." Although a seven-foot hawk is an intimidating figure, his demeanor offsets any potential discomfort. His presence has a remarkable gentleness; it is light and easy with a calming effect.

One morning as I was studying the Word and praying in the Spirit, I became aware of the presence of the Council of Angels, but they were all still and silent. The Hawk-Angel manifested more prominently, so I turned my attention towards him. The silent language was coming off him and he said, "This is why I am here. This is part of what I do. He will cleanse His bride. She will be without spot or wrinkle or any such thing: to sanctify, to cleanse, and to wash her, that she would be holy and without blemish. And every man that has this hope in him purifies himself even as He is pure. This is that. It is the sovereign work of the Spirit in you and among you, and we also do His work. We (the Hawk-Angels) eat the dead things from your lives as they are highlighted by the Spirit, and as you are ready to release them, casting your cares on Him, to be freed from their burden."

(I have seen these hawk angels pulling the dead flesh of the carnal man even from the chests of people yielding to the Lord, and then eating it like black, rotten meat. The Lord told me this will make room for the growth of the new man.)

"Yes, this is the cross of Christ working in your life. We take part in this as an operation of the Spirit. That is why I am telling you. We are helping you all. It will free you all further so you may walk in greater intimacy with Him, and so the power of the Spirit may flow through you all in greater measure to lift up others for His name's sake. For Christ did not come to be served, but to serve others. This is that in you all. This death works in you, so that life may be expressed through you to others. This is part of the mission of the hawks as servants of the Spirit. We have been doing this work even before you were made aware. We are making you aware so that others may be comforted through this knowledge.

"Your Heavenly Father does provide for you. He has us intimately involved with all of you in this way. Remind the people that we also carry the entreating heart of the Spirit that pleads with you to keep your hearts open to God and allow this inner working to continue. We are here to help glorify His name in all of you and through all of you."

The Hawk Angel looked at me and then switched to speaking through his mouth, "I am a Captain among us (the Hawk Angels). We move freely through the spirit realm wherever we are needed. You will also move freely through the spirit realm. You are being trained. Standing in your place is a key. Let your soul be comforted. For though the fire rages within you and upon you, you still have full access to Him, and to His peace with joy. In fact, the hottest furnace is a safe place, for the Son of God can appear there and live

> "THE GROUND WILL SHAKE AS WE MOVE AMONG YOU. THERE WILL BE NEW HOPE AND NEW FAITH. BREAK FREE OF THE CHAINS THAT BIND. CONSECRATE THE PEOPLE. A PEOPLE SEPARATED TO THE LORD WITH FRESH SINGLENESS OF MIND AND PURPOSE."

IN THE COUNSEL OF ANGELS

there with you. And He will sustain your life. Remember, it is for love that He calls all of you, and for you it is to give you His charge. Remember when you were told that we would lay down a circle of fire around this house?"

As the hawk angel spoke, I recalled the prophecy he was referring to. It was from nearly two years ago. His silent language told me to find the memo where I recorded that session and prophecy. I searched my records and found it—a vision about flaming horses, chariots, and angels. I recalled that at that time I thought the circle of fire was one of protection around the body of Christ. But the captain corrected me, and gave the intended meaning. The vision also stated, "The ground will shake as we move among you. There will be new hope and new faith. Break free of the chains that bind. Consecrate the people. A people separated to the Lord with fresh singleness of mind and purpose."

The captain informed me that the vision is a prophecy of the work that the Hawk Angels perform among us. In this regard, their work is much like those who would weed out a garden, so the weeds don't choke out the good plants or steal life-giving nutrients from the soil. And we are the planting of the Lord. Although the hawk angels are equipped to see our every fault, there is no judgment in them. There is only gentleness and entreaty, with the intent that all would receive the Spirit's help to be renewed, and that no one be written off or be left behind. The Spirit says, "Come".

COMMANDERS OF ARMIES

These two Commanders of Armies and their assignments are as unique and different as could be. One commands rapid-deployment shock troops for short mission surgical strikes, like unseating a demonic power or tearing down a spiritual stronghold. The other commands a massive assault and occupation force; they are more like a kingdom steamroller against our enemy.

Commander One–Special Operations

This angel's name means "the kingdom will flourish." He appears as a regal young prince with wings. He commands sixty legions with 6,000 angels apiece; they are special operations strike forces. He promised I would go with them to see them at work, and that has definitely been the case.

Here is how he introduced himself. An angel Battle Commander presented himself to me one day, shortly after Karen and I arrived at a little house near Mt. Hood for a short holiday. I spoke in tongues nearly the whole drive up there. In my spirit I knew there was something new and different for us just up ahead.

As soon as we got to the cabin, the angel showed himself to me, and I understood he wanted to interact. I mentioned to Karen there were a bunch of angels present. She already knew, and commented they were there for us. Once the car was unloaded, I got my journal and sat down to listen. (The angels are very patient with us; they understand time, and our needs

IN THE COUNSEL OF ANGELS

and responsibilities in the natural world.)

As soon as I sat down, the angel immediately made contact again. He appeared as a young man—except for the wings, of course. He was vibrant, with youthful energy; engaging, and profoundly regal. I felt as though I was in the presence of a fearless, young prince. His demeanor was not at all demanding or intimidating, but he certainly felt like royalty. Just being near him made me want to snap to attention. His shoulder-length brown hair brushed against the glimmering white robe with gold trim that he wore.

His spirit-to-spirit language was already speaking. I sensed he could open doors that no man could open. He was a persuader of men. Previously the angels had told me, "Our ministry has now become your ministry."

Angels carry God's delegated power and authority. They can support us with their gifts and attributes, even causing their words and influence to work upon and through us as an operation of the Holy Spirit, who is their on-earth Supervisor. Demons aren't the only spirits that can influence people. The rebellion in Satan and his demons has made them perverse and unclean in nature and influence. The nature of God's angels is holy, and their ministry is pure. What the angels carry is what they give out. Who they are is a part of what they impart.

The house we were staying in is in a neighborhood built among a beautiful evergreen forest not far from the base of Mount Hood. Our first night, as Karen and I sat around our campfire in the back yard, many angels landed on the ground all around us and showed themselves in the spirit; it was such an obvious and powerful presence. They too were dressed in white robes with gold trim; evidently, it was their leader I met yesterday, for they were dressed just like him. I felt they numbered in the many thousands.

Our second night, we were again around the campfire, and the newly revealed angels showed themselves again. It felt much like you would expect when being surrounded by an angel army. They bring "heaven-culture" to earth to influence and change us. I could now tell they were a legion numbering around 6.000, but I sensed this number to be open-ended. I wondered if there were additional legions with this group, but not present and not yet revealed? The commander, sometime later, disclosed that he commands 360,000 troops, which is a total of sixty legions.

<u>Commander Two-Occupation Forces</u>

This angel's name means "Heavy Infantry." He is a commander of occupation forces. He is eight feet tall, maybe 400 or 500 earth-pounds. He is a serious-minded commanding officer. There is a power, a capacity to conduct heavenly violence, that radiates from him that is intimidating. No doubt, he is a terror to the forces of darkness. He stands in the circle, just to my left. Holy Spirit has indicated this angel completes the Council Circle at a total of eight.

This particular angel has spoken out loud to me only twice. When he speaks, I feel like I am melting. So much authority and power are in his words that my strength is instantly depleted; once, it even partially closed off my throat, nearly taking my breath away. Perhaps this is why he rarely speaks aloud. He scares me, in an awe-struck sort of way.

> The fear of the LORD is clean, enduring forever.
> Psalm 19:9a.

IN THE COUNSEL OF ANGELS

The terror this being carries is, of course, something he releases when he engages the enemy.

Upon his initial arrival, his silent language was speaking. He told me that he brought with him heavy infantry, occupation troops ready for hand-to-hand combat with the enemy. Millions were with him; twenty-five million to be exact (that is somewhere between 4200-5000 Legions). I had felt an unusual, looming weight high in the sky overhead in the spirit that day over the whole western side of our region. It wasn't a bad thing at all, just unfamiliar. I had been speaking in new tongues a lot beginning that day, and then this happened.

"New tongues for new realms," the angels said, "and new angelic operations." I understood that it was the presence of this massive force of holy angels coming down into our atmosphere from above.

Then the commander spoke aloud, "You cannot see my mission or my forces now because the Lord has concealed them from sight."

His forces and their operations remain a mystery to me to this day.

LION ANGEL GENERAL

The wicked flee when no one is pursuing, but the righteous are bold as a lion. Proverbs 28:1, NAS.

The commanding General and Overseer of all angelic operations for the Greater Portland/Vancouver Metro Area (GPVMA), and beyond is a Lion Angel. I know that because the Lion-Angel General told me so. His name means "rich and kingly." He appears just a bit larger than an earthly lion. I have seen him walk on two feet, upright like a man walks, and on all fours. This angel is not one of the eight who stand in my Council Circle. However, he is one I receive counsel and input from, as he will come to me from time to time with an update of his operations, and with instructions for me.

Here is how the Lion General introduced himself to me. It was Sunday evening service at church. I was hoping to see what the Lord was doing with His angels as they ministered to the body this night. But the Lord preferred that I be ministered to instead. Many prayed for me, including Pastor Arlan, and I was impacted by the Holy Spirit with peace and encouragement. As Pastor Barbro prayed I also received infilling of the Spirit, and I began to roar like a lion. This was, in fact, the third time this had happened when she has prayed for me. Yes, I thought this to be a bit strange, but I had yielded myself to the Spirit of God, so I trusted Him and went with it. During this time a lion appeared in the spirit on the stage behind me. The Holy Spirit told me to go and kneel in front of him. I turned, climbed on the stage, and knelt near the lion. In my spirit I knew I was not to worship him, so I understood this was not a form of the Lord Jesus that I was seeing. The lion looked me in the eye but said nothing. He began to walk towards me in slow motion. When he got to me, I watched as he walked right inside of me and disappeared. I did not see him go out the back of me. He was simply gone. This happened before I began to understand how to interpret angelic impartations.

The next time I saw this Lion Angel was a few days later during my morning prayer time. My Lead Angel showed up, and he brought with him the Lion Angel I saw Sunday night at church. The lion was standing, this time on his two hind feet. The angels told me to stand up and face them toe to toe. As we stood toe to toe and eye to eye, I was terrified. My flesh was literally crawling with goose bumps that moved in waves across my skin. My strength drained away. Never had I felt like that before. I wanted to run. The only thing holding me there was discipline and a desire to be obedient to Holy Spirit.

The Lion Angel began to speak. He said, "I am the righteousness of God. I bring the fire. We will set up camp on this house, and on this hill." (Our church property is on a hill and near its top.) "It has begun. We serve the same Lord. We have come to glorify His name and distribute His glory. Many companies have come. We are in charge now. Pound the drum of worship. Pound the drum of deliverance."

Several times his silent language told me to look at his face. He had all the facial features of a natural lion, but his bright green eyes shone with a deep, heavenly intelligence. Flames

moved across his face from the inside of his body. For some reason I said to him, "We have not seen many miracles yet."

He replied, "What is a miracle? It is His kingdom come, His will being done, in earth as it is in heaven." I understood he had spoken with a double meaning attached to his words. He was instructing that the Spirit wants us to pray this part of the Lord's Prayer, and pray that our hearts would beat as one body, along with the angels according to that prayer. This prayer then, is an apostolic directive from our Lord and a kingdom key, guiding us to align with the Lord in His purpose and His will: His kingdom come, His will be done.

The Lion Angel continued, "I am the righteousness of God. I bring the fire. Be steadfast. Look only forward."

I stood in electrified silence for what seemed like a long time. I could tell the angels were about to leave. He spoke once more, "You will see the Lord. If you think you are terrified of me, just wait until you meet the One who has all power." Then both angels vanished.

Angels know what you have been thinking. On another occasion the Lion Angel General came to me asked, "Is it really so strange to think that speaking with angels is reality? Who do you consider to be more truthful, men or God's angels? If we have failed you, then you are free to doubt us." He spoke this challenge with great kindness, knowing he was relieving some of my doubts. I knelt down and leaned into him to receive his comfort. It was so peaceful. Lions are good snugglers! In a while, I felt the angels dismiss me from our meeting.

It was my morning prayer time as I sat in my reading chair in our living room. The Lion Angel General appeared to me. He was standing in flames as he walked through the wall and entered the room. Then he said, "Watch. Watch and see what the fire of the Lord will do." He took a couple more steps and then both of us were at my church in Portland, which is about twenty miles from my house. We were standing in the parking lot, near where the angel encampment is located. There were flames twenty to thirty feet high here and there throughout their camp. The flames begin on the ground, but the fire did not burn anything up. The Lion Angel General walked on all fours through the angel camp and then over to the east side of the church building. He turned his head suddenly towards the building and crouched like a cat ready to lunge. He opened his mouth and a powerful blast of flames shot out. The flames went the whole distance through the length of the building and continued onto the outer patio on the West side. Like with the other flames, it looked like nothing was burned up after he was done. He was marvelous in this display of God's glory. He really does act as the express will of God.

He turned to me and said, "You are not your own. You are bought with a price, the precious blood of Christ. How does it feel to be at the center of His will?"

I told him I was humbled and grateful beyond words. Then he said, "Let's go inside." We walked into the entry at the West entrance. As we went through the double doors into the sanctuary, I could see it was all a radiant white. There were beams and columns and ornate carvings that do not exist in the natural. It was all white like stone, yet it felt warm like ivory. Though there was no visible light source, everything was sparkling and glistening. He said to me, "There are no more shadows in here."

He was right. I also understood his double meaning; he was

talking of the room and about people's hearts. There would be repentance, confession of faults, cleansing and deliverance, and the freedom of walking in His light and having fellowship with one another. He was very patient with me. He knew I was overwhelmed, and he let me take it all in at my pace. The sanctuary felt more like it was part of heaven, rather than on this earth.

The Lion then said, "It begins here but it will quickly spread. Now the 'dark one' (the chief demonic principality over the GPVMA) knows his rule is threatened. His time is very short. You call this the 'Sunset Highway' (referring to nearby Highway 26). I call it the 'Corridor of His Fire.'"

This encounter left me spiritually and physically exhausted, and the angel knew it. A weighty presence came over me, warmth flooded my chest, and suddenly my strength returned. The Lion continued, "Let the wineskins of your spirits stretch and expand. Take it all in. Be flexible in the Lord and though you stretch, you will not burst. This is new life we bring. The same Spirit, but life you have not known. Write it down. In this life-stream is also contained the call for others to come. It is the Father's heart to draw all men to Him. The fresh gifts will fall like rain now. They are part of the new life. Don't worry about how big this will get. Your shepherds are already prepared. Tell them we are happy for them that this joy has come to you."

ANGELS OF MERCY

> And He was in the wilderness forty days being tempted by Satan; and He was with the wild beasts, and the angels were ministering to Him.
> Mark 1:13, NAS.

This was a severe testing for Christ, with real temptations; but praise God, Jesus did not yield to the devil. Instead, our Champion prevailed against the evil one, and emerged from that fight in the power of the Spirit.

We are not told specifically how the angels ministered to Jesus. Did they give Jesus strength, comfort, encouragement, food and water, spiritual nourishment? When angels come to minister, they show up to take care of specific needs from God's point of view. We can be certain the angels were effective in their ministry to Jesus. It was a display of the Father's mercy.

I have seen angels ministering to people: laying their hands on them, comforting them, moving them around, and even performing miraculous surgeries and healings.

EARLY ENCOUNTERS

One Sunday evening during a ministry time, the pastors at Westside Vineyard were praying over many of us and declaring transformation and more grace. I was on my knees and felt a

distinct pain over my heart. It did not cause me concern, but it did get my attention.

Just then my spiritual eyes were opened, and I saw one of the first angels ever to contact me. He was kneeling right in front of me, and his right hand was pushing on the left side of my chest just above my heart. With his left hand he held out a knife which looked like a fine ceremonial dagger and he presented it to me with grace and dignity. He made me feel like I was the special one, and not him. The double-edged blade was shiny, like highly polished fine steel; the handle appeared like carved ivory with golden rivets. I began to receive understanding through silent, spirit-to-spirit language from the angel to me.

The dagger represented the word of knowledge that makes an incision into peoples' hurting hearts. It pierces through the scar tissue, all the way to the very depth of their original wound—the source of all their unresolved pain and festering infection. I was told that this opens an opportunity to pour in the oil of joy for gladness; for a merry heart does good, like a medicine. Later, I came to understand that the word of knowledge, the gift of prophecy, and declarations of the promises of God, all working together, create a very potent combination indeed.

Operating this way brings relief from a person's misery, and sets them free into a life-changing, deeper revelation of God's love and care for them. The double-edge of the dagger symbolizes that this is also a gift of impartation. Those who are healed will become healers of others. Our Lord is the God of multiplication.

I was completely surprised by this visitation. Clearly, the

IN THE COUNSEL OF ANGELS

Lord chose to override my doubt and unbelief regarding things of this nature. There's that grace again! You might think that I would rush to tell someone of my angelic encounter, but I did just the opposite. I told no one about it for many weeks; my doubting mind did not want to risk being mistaken, or to look like a "crazy dreamer."

It is a miracle that I even recorded the account in my journal.

≈

During worship service one night I went to the back of the sanctuary to worship there. I was watching as I worshiped. An angel walked the length of the sanctuary towards me. I knew he was one of the Angels of Mercy. The Captain of the Angels of Mercy had already contacted me that night, letting me know they would be working. This other angel walked up and stood in front of me, but off to the side a little. He did not speak; typical angel etiquette. I studied his appearance for a few moments. He appeared in a highly detailed, black outline with translucent silvery shadings in between. I could see his facial features clearly and distinctly. He had swirling designs or markings on his face, a full beard, and long, dark brown hair.

I approached him. "What are you guys doing here?"

His demeanor was casual, relaxed, and deliberate. He replied in English, "We are here to help relieve you (plural) of grief and regrets. They can be a hindrance to your faith."

I could feel in his words the weight of the priority the Spirit has placed on seeing us grow in faith in this season, and in this new realm of operation.

"You are all focusing on receiving your upgrades, and that's good. But you are not stopping here. You are on the move, and

there is so much more for you."

That's it. We are a people on the move. The Spirit is growing the body of Christ into the image of Christ. We are moving away from identifying with the image of the earthly (hence the relieving of grief and regrets that could hinder by tying us to earthly cares), and towards walking in the image of the heavenly, the mystery that is being revealed, which is Christ in us, the hope of glory.

OUR SWEET LORD JESUS

> Jesus, knowing that the Father had given all things into His hands, and that He had come from God and was going to God, rose from supper and laid aside His garments, took a towel and girded Himself. After that, He poured water into a basin and began to wash the disciples' feet, and to wipe them with the towel with which He was girded.
> John 13:3-5, NKJ.

Jesus' ultimate act of humility for our sakes was seen when He humbled Himself and became obedient to the point of death, even the death of the cross. The above Scripture displays His humility prior to the cross, as He showed the apostles how we, His body, should treat one another. These demonstrations of humility from the Son of God are a perfect representation of the humility in God's eternal nature.

Here are a few times when the Lord Jesus showed up in the spirit, both to hang out and to talk about the Father's business. Though He is the resurrected and glorified Christ, Jesus is also humble beyond my comprehension; He is so NOT into Himself. It has been a total eye-opener for me to be with Jesus when He comes in this way; our Savior, older brother, and friend. Jesus approached in the spirit while I was meeting with the Council of Angels. He was just outside our circle near the four-o'clock position. As He stepped to move inside the circle, my

IN THE COUNSEL OF ANGELS

Lead Angel and one of the Battalion Commanders softened their stances to let Him pass between them. As Jesus brushed between them, He put a hand on each of their shoulders, the way a friend gestures to say, "Thanks for letting me through." It thrilled my heart to see the warmth, gentleness, and humility of Jesus in action. Though He is Creator of all, He really enjoys interacting with us as one of us. He stopped in the middle of the circle and looked at me. Then He nodded His head at me and said, "Thank you."

I told Him, "I can't do this without You"; to which He replied, "Then do not try. Remember, hand to hand, friend to friend, face to face." Tears began to come to my eyes and I continued to look at Him.

Then Jesus surprised me again by asking, "What do you want?"

I felt like He was handing me a blank check, and I did not want to blow it. I thought and searched my heart for what seemed like a long time. Then I answered, "I want to be with You, and I also want to make a difference."

Jesus said, "Remember I knew you all before you ever came into your bodies on this earth. Every one of you I knew before sin had touched you." (I could feel His eternalness and His divine love in those words.) I said I was sorry that I get impatient with His plans and timings.

He said sympathetically, "It is to be expected, for patience must be learned. Run your race as fast as the Spirit will take you, but no faster." Even though He chose to come into view humbly as the Son of man, still it would be so easy for me to bow down, kiss His feet, and worship.

On another occasion, I sensed the presence of the Lord

Jesus manifesting near me, but His presence was so faint I could easily have dismissed the impression and continued right on by. I turned to Jesus and asked, "Why do You come to me like this, so subtly?" His answer was unexpected.

"Because I can trust you. You will not bend Our plans to your liking. Remember, be filled with the Spirit. You cannot do My work without Him. But with Him everything comes together just as it should. When you enter a new realm for the kingdom you will want to be filled with the Spirit. Otherwise, you do risk being so spiritually dull you might miss the advantage being given to you. Do you see how much My peoples' minds are not set on the things above? It is because the affections of the soul have not been shifted away from the earthly things.

"The appetites of the body are rightly fed with the fruit of this world. The appetites of the spirit and soul are to be nourished with the things of My kingdom. The soul is to learn the new ways, and to hunger for the kingdom. It is a mismatch and a gross misunderstanding to try and feed the needs of the spirit man with the things of this world. This practice must end. My body must mature and rise in the power of the Spirit. Some clutch their pet projects, beliefs, and expressions thinking they possess kingdom secrets; for the mind of the flesh is protective of self-interests. But when a kingdom secret is revealed, it is free to all who would receive. Some have mistakenly settled for crumbs. They hide what they have in a shell to protect it from loss. But it is those who have who will receive more, and they find an abundance. They wish to share and bid others to come and eat.

"So continue to freely give. Accelerate your giving, so that

My blessing in your life may increase as well. Kingdom rule is with the open heart. This is why you must love your enemies. It is also why you must stay close. And the One who teaches you is inside you. Trust in Him and the path laid out for you. He will direct your course. If you will continue to follow Me, you will be astounded by where I take you. You must stay close, so you will know I am your Source, and the One leading you. Now go and leaven the whole lump with what I have given you. Bear one another's burdens; my children are to be free."

ANGELS AND INTERCESSORS: ALIGNING IN WAR

MINISTERING SPIRITS SENT FORTH TO MINISTER

Are they not all ministering spirits sent forth to minister for those who will inherit salvation?
Hebrews 1:14, NKJ.

The ministry of angels in the earth is that they are heavenly ministering spirits sent forth by God to minister to us—those who will inherit salvation. Through the angelic encounters orchestrated by the Holy Spirit, my heart's cry—as well as the prayer that Mariyamma, guest minister from India had prayed, "show him Your will, my Master"—was now being answered. Had it not been for the revelations showing me the unlimited abundance of heaven's resources available to fulfill the Father's promise to Jesus, I may have had difficulty believing what God wanted to do through His intercessors and saints. In truth, the Lord of hosts is with us, as are His ministering spirits He sends forth. We can be incredibly grateful for the ministry of angels.

The God of Angel Armies is fulfilling His promise to Jesus.

> "Ask of Me, and I will give You the nations for Your inheritance, and the ends of the earth for Your

IN THE COUNSEL OF ANGELS

> possession. You shall break them with a rod of iron; You shall dash them to pieces like a potter's vessel." Psalm 2:8-9, NKJ.

The demonic principalities and powers currently holding false claim to the heavens are being unseated and thrown down in the authority of Christ Jesus (more about that in a moment). Shortly after our introduction in my prayer closet, my Lead Angel began speaking about throwing down the senior demonic principality over Portland, Oregon. Honestly, at the time this was something that I really knew nothing about experientially in my spirit man. It was clear I would engage in this assignment with Holy Spirit by faith, or I would not be able to engage in it at all.

The Lord's upgrade in my life has meant that Holy Spirit is actively raising me up and propelling me into a truly broad and "extraordinarily spacious" new frontier in the heavenly realms. This is a partial fulfillment on an experiential level of the positional truth in His declaration to us:

> And He raised us up together and seated us together in the heavenly realms in Christ Jesus." Ephesians 2:6, BLB.

Big God, big kingdom, big resources.

From the very beginning of this assignment from Jesus with the angels I had the sense that I was being integrated into the army of God's intercessors at a fresh and heightened level of revelation and activity. The understanding of this continues to unfold and develop. This is evident on a practical level in part as the Lord continues to unite me in spirit and in communication with so many individuals near and far who are walking in their kingdom assignments from Holy Spirit. I was informed that the Master's will for me was to partner with saints and angels as an intercessor for the tearing down of great and ancient strongholds of satan. Also, I was told that I would help the body learn to work with the angels in fulfilling this promise.

READ THE THRONES

And he carried me away in the Spirit... Revelation 17:3, NAS.

One day my Lead Angel took me up with him in the spirit into the skies above earth. We must have been tens of thousands of feet in the air. I think we were near the upper limits of the troposphere, for there were thick clouds below us but no clouds visible above us. I was riding on the angel's back as we flew just above the tops of the clouds. It was not cold around me and the air was comfortable and breathable. Although we were flying, there was no wind-resistance, nor were there any G-forces evident. The angel did not flap his wings to fly but seemed to glide to wherever he wanted.

I noticed a huge dark hole in some clouds just below us. I said to the angel, "What is that?"

He turned his head back towards me and said, "It is a dark Throne. You are not to fear them." The angel's use of "throne" refers to a heavenly being with jurisdictional power and influence over a certain area.

Up ahead I could see another dark hole in the clouds. The holes were shaped like funnels; large and round at the top, tapering inward as they went down into the darkness inside the cloud. This one had some kind of black structure down inside.

The angel looked back and said, "I want you to learn how

to recognize and read the Thrones. You will not always engage them. But you will read them." This was the very beginning of my training from the angels on the discerning of demonic principalities.

The Holy Spirit has continued the training process, teaching me to "read" the nature and influence of principalities, both godly ones and demonic ones. The godly Thrones either come to me, or I am taken to them. I spend time in their presence listening to them as they communicate with me, and I observe their actions and behavior. When the Spirit takes me into the presence of demonic Thrones, I am usually escorted by a massive force of angels. When it is for reconnaissance, they bring me very close, and I watch and listen. When it is for battle, I observe the activity usually from a distance. Sometimes however, Holy Spirit has me participate in the operations with bold declarations of words He gives me at the time.

TROOP DEPLOYMENT OPERATIONS

> And it came to pass, when Joshua was by Jericho, that he lifted his eyes and looked, and behold, a man stood opposite him with his sword drawn in his hand. And Joshua went to him and said to him, "Are you for us or for our adversaries? So he said, "No, but as Commander of the army of the Lord I have now come. And Joshua fell on his face to the earth and worshiped, and said to him, "What does my lord say to his servant? Then the Commander of the Lord's army said to Joshua, "Take your sandal off your foot, for the place where you stand is holy." And Joshua did so. Joshua 5: 13-15, NKJ

Here we see Joshua coming face to face with the realization that God's Angel Armies were with him; one of the fulfillments of God's promise to him.

> "No man will be able to stand before you all the days of your life. Just as I have been with Moses, I will be with you; I will not fail you or forsake you."
> Joshua 1:5, NAS.

God's angels had been with Moses when he confronted Pharaoh in Egypt and released the plagues—and even before that with the burning bush. Joshua had been with Moses and the children of Israel in Egypt and had experienced many visitations of the Lord, and had encountered His Presence, His glory, His wrath, and His angels. Also, Joshua had been with Moses many times at the Tent of Meeting in the wilderness, when God would come down in the pillar of cloud. Now, the Commander's presence made it clear to Joshua that the angels were with him as well. No doubt, Joshua's spiritual discernment was well-developed. Being sharp and keen, he immediately acknowledged the Commander of the Lord's army, and responded by bowing his heart and his body.

I was studying the Word and praying when an angel descended in the spirit and presented himself to me. When he landed, I could see it was one of the angels from my Council. Never before had I seen him enter like that. He had always just manifested from his place in the Council circle. (Sometime later, after the vision, I realized he had just come from the place in the heavens where they were about to take me. He descended to get me because they were ready for me.) The angel began speaking to me. I knew it was instruction but I have no memory of what he said. This is uncharacteristic, as I am usually listening to the angels speak to me in their languages, and then I write the interpretation in English into my journal. Later it became clear to me that it was during these moments the Holy Spirit caught me away with them, though I did not realize or remember any of this until after I returned and the Spirit later revealed it to me. I was taken to a platform in space; a flat surface suspended in the air measuring about fifteen feet by twenty feet. Two angels from my Council stood there with me: the one who came to get me and my Lead Angel. As I looked at the view of sky around us and saw that we were well above the clouds below, I supposed we were up in the earth's

IN THE COUNSEL OF ANGELS

stratosphere, a place where so many angel armies are staged as they await their Earth assignments. The stratosphere is also just above the upper limits of the angelic warfare zone over earth.

At times I was viewing the vision from the third-person vantage point where, as if at a distance, I watched myself interact with the angels. This alternated between the typical first-person position, where I was conversing with the angels face to face. Angels came and landed on the platform and we talked. Sometimes as many as four to five angels at a time came and joined us. I knew they were all commanders of armies and their senior officers. The angel commanders were speaking to me in angel languages and I was speaking back to them, also in angel languages. This is the first time I recall speaking with them in that fashion. Though I was obviously fluent in their languages, I have no details or recollection about what we had discussed during these operations. We would talk a while and then they would leave. Often right before they left the platform, I would say something while pointing in a direction. I understood these were troop-deployment operations that we were discussing. I watched as the officers left the platform and went back to rejoin their armies. Then, in a flash and streaks of light, that army would move out at light speed and be gone. This scenario repeated over and over and over again for what seemed like many, many hours. It was like being at a job and working a very long shift, though there was no way to track the actual passing of time. There were countless millions of angels involved in these operations.

Sometime after I returned from the vision, my wife told me that I had been gone for two or three days. To be clear, I had still been physically present at our house with her, but she says it was like my soul was no longer very present, and clearly my attention was somewhere else. I had no memories of being at home or of any earthly activities for those days; only memories of being with the angels.

I came away from the vision with a few clear impressions. I understood these angel armies were being released not just for our Portland area, but also to areas all over North America, from one end of the continent to the other. One of my strongest recollections was that the atmosphere we were in was saturated with the intercessory prayers of God's people. This is the real purpose for telling this story. The intercessory prayers and heart-cries of God's people are living things and are at the leading edge of these operations of the Holy Spirit and His angels. I could also hear the heart cries of the lost rising up from the earth and calling out for God. Not only did I hear these two types of cries, but I also felt them as an atmospheric presence all around us. The prayers of the saints were combining with the cries of the lost. The two cries blended as a sort of song; like a melody and counterpoint that was other-worldly, both wonderful and eerie. I could tell the angels were also well aware of these cries in the atmosphere. I believe these angel operations are a direct response from God to the cries from the peoples on the earth.

> THE INTERCESSORY PRAYERS AND HEART-CRIES OF GOD'S PEOPLE ARE LIVING THINGS AND ARE AT THE LEADING EDGE OF THESE OPERATIONS OF THE HOLY SPIRIT AND HIS ANGELS.

God's heart has been touched with your prayers and intercessions, and He is answering with corresponding actions by sending His armies. This is part of the reason God has allowed me to see into these unseen realities; that you who pray into His interests would know He is working, and what some of His activities look like, even if you are not seeing these things yourself. Sometime after I returned from the vision, I recalled the moment when the angel brought me back. He said, "God is causing His kingdom to descend upon the earth. The world is being shaken wherever the kingdom approaches and enforces its rule. Light disturbs, displaces, and dispels the darkness."

REGIONAL ANGELIC ACTIVITY: TO FREE A REGION

A wise man scales the city of the mighty and pulls down the stronghold in which they trust.
Proverbs 21:22, BSB.

God is continuing to release angel armies who will affect cities, regions, and even whole nations. I continue to have contact from angelic commanders and messengers who report on these types of activities. Here is a visitation I had one night, which happened the instant before I fell asleep. I am including details of how it occurred to help you feel some of the otherworldliness of the encounter.

> THE PRAYERS OF THE SAINTS WERE COMBINING WITH THE CRIES OF THE LOST. THE TWO CRIES BLENDED AS A SORT OF SONG; LIKE A MELODY AND COUNTERPOINT THAT WAS OTHER-WORLDLY, BOTH WONDERFUL AND EERIE.

The ceiling of my bedroom and roof opened and revealed an expanse of sky and deep space. An angel quickly descended out of the heavens and stopped a distance above me. Clearly, he was a mighty warrior commander. He was so regal, I wondered if he was perhaps a prince among the angels. He told me he brought with him 200 legions of

IN THE COUNSEL OF ANGELS

angels who are nation changers. (It was understood between the angel and me that these armies were being released in response to prayers, petitions, and intercessions offered to God from His people. People are continually engaged in targeted prayer for the kingdom to come to earth, and our heavenly Father responds with His armies.) The commander's angelic forces were sent to take down demonic princes and rulers that empower men and women who stand as wicked leaders in their spheres of influence in our world and cultures. These angels also expose the hidden works of darkness in the world of men. Every hidden thing will be uncovered. Then they enforce the kingdom and serve to influence the atmosphere with God's righteousness and justice. This angel certainly must be just one of many angel army commanders that God has released for these purposes.

The next morning, I had no recollection that this visitation had even occurred. Later in the day the Spirit reminded me of the visitation. It was like experiencing a memory of something that you don't recall ever occurring. I did then recall the instant before I had fallen asleep when the angel appeared, but the rest of what the Spirit showed me with the angel I had to take by faith the word from the Spirit of Truth, because I had no memory of the details of the event.

On another day, an angel reported, "You have sensed more fighting locally. We have been as thunder exploding down on the enemy. He is well-entrenched in the heart of this city. The darkness is woven in and through the power structures of men. These battles are not over quickly. If we ended them quickly, men would die. We hit the enemy and it softens his hold on men. We hit the enemy again and he is forced to retract his influence and retreat, and so on. This is part of the process to free a region. It is much like your chemotherapy treatments; attack the disease, but don't kill the patient. Where do you think man's science got that wisdom and strategy from anyway? We are fighting now some of the most evil and powerful demons in the region. They are killers. We do not want to show this to you. But we have allowed you to sense it, and you have been praying into it with us, as have many others."

TAKING DOWN A SATANIC PRINCE

> Let the high praises of God be in their mouth, and a two-edged sword in their hand, to execute vengeance on the nations, and punishments on the peoples; to bind their kings with chains, and their nobles with fetters of iron; to execute on them the written judgment. This honor have all His saints. Psalm 149:6-9, NKJ.

The angel of the Lord was releasing his information to me about a local, satanic "ruling" prince, which turned out to be the senior demonic principality over Portland, Oregon. The angel said that assaulting the demon prince would be a key. Holy Spirit began to direct me to use the information from the angel to declare and oppose this evil principality.

Under the Holy Spirit's authorization, I commanded that the evil spirit reveal itself; I challenged its authority in the authority of the name of Jesus, and bound it in the heavens from here on earth. Over the course of many visits from this angel and updates about this operation I became assured that Holy Spirit had summoned many prayer warriors to take part in this fight. During this series of visits the angel had also said, "Your words of faith will strike these stones (in the spirit), and we will carry out the attacks. This dark one will rise to oppose you. He will tempt you. You will resist him by seeking the lowest place. In that place of humility, the Lord's hosts will be a cover over you. During this assault, your enemy will expose himself, and warrior angels will vanquish him. There is a great heavenly host amassed for this engagement. The angel of God's righteousness waits to sit upon the throne, once the dark one has fallen. The purifying fire is here. It is a terrible thing to fall into the hands of the living God. Know the times and understand His ways. Those who count themselves as "all in" will in no way be cast out. This is His will and plan, read to you off the pages in this book. God is placing His glory in earthen vessels because He wants to. He is activating His chosen, and you will operate as one: one in Spirit, one in mind, one in purpose: many members, many functions, but one Lord. The refiner's fire is upon the house."

Morning prayer time on this day began with thanking and praising God with understanding and in the spirit. My tongue changed to one I had not heard before. Then I was in the spirit in a place where the sky was dark, and a large satanic angel was hovering nearby; a demonic dragon who must have been four times my size. He was angry and threatening, grotesque and ugly; pure evil. Silently I asked Holy Spirit for His guidance. Then I demanded of this creature, "Who are you?"

He replied, "I am the displaced dark one." He kept moving around and making threatening gestures and facial expressions at me. It seemed like he wanted to harm me, but I sensed that unseen forces were preventing him.

I quoted Scriptures as they came to my spirit and continued to speak in tongues. I told this evil one, "I am submitted to God the Father, Jesus Christ, the Holy Spirit, and God's authority in the church. I am covered by the blood of the Lamb, as are those of my house, and of my church. Now be bound in chains and

IN THE COUNSEL OF ANGELS

thrown into the pit." Instantly he vanished from sight. (I later learned that the angels had bound him in chains.) Groans and other strange noises from deep in my spirit were being voiced, as if being squeezed out of my insides. After a while I felt release as the intercessory burden was satisfied and lifted away. I thought how fitting that God would throw down this dark power on Good Friday.

After this encounter, I was filled with thankfulness. I told God I want His heart inside of me. I want to look and act like Jesus, whatever it takes. This operation was all part of God being glorified in the earth. To Him be glory in the church by Christ Jesus to all generations forever and ever.

THE THREE THRONES OF PORTLAND

To bring to light what is the administration of the mystery which for ages has been hidden in God who created all things; so that the manifold wisdom of God might now be made known through the church to the rulers and the authorities in the heavenly places,
Ephesians 3:9-10.

The following events took place during 2016 and 2017. These things occurred during a time when God was accelerating me into areas of the unseen realm and levels of my walk with Him that were previously unknown to me. My assignment has continued and I am on a learning curve that often seems near vertical due to the newness and vastness of the realms in the spirit and the uniqueness of nearly every encounter. For me, acclimating to this kind of activity in the spirit realm has been a continual process of stretching and growing in faith, and trusting in the Lord. All that I share is, of course, just glimpses and snapshots of a monumental and complex master plan orchestrated by the wisdom and the hand of our Almighty God.

When my Lead Angel first began speaking about God throwing down the senior demonic principality over Portland, he explained that God would afterward establish His rule by installing His own Thrones to rule here. The angel said,

IN THE COUNSEL OF ANGELS

"Fight, push, pray, preach. The angel of God's righteousness will sit upon the throne, once the dark one has fallen. The city will have a new slogan, 'Keep Portland Blessed.'" (The city's counter-cultural slogan has been 'Keep Portland Weird.' I much prefer the new slogan!)

I can report that the mighty and holy angelic Throne is now seated and ruling on behalf of the kingdom of heaven in the heavenlies over the Greater Portland/Vancouver Metro Area. As to the senior demonic principality, God's angels dethroned it and took it away; a story for another time, perhaps. God's senior Throne is, as promised, raining down righteousness over his new dominion of the region. I have seen this happening like rings of light pulsating from beneath his throne high in the skies. The light rings radiate out in ever-enlarging circles in all directions as they approach the ground. They extend outward and contact the ground in the region to the North around Woodland, Washington; to the South around Woodburn, Oregon; to the East around Troutdale, Oregon; and to the West around Forest Grove, Oregon. This influence will not stop but will increase in intensity. It is working to slowly familiarize "all flesh" in the area with the Lord's glorious presence. This is influencing the spirit of the mind in many, many people, and setting them up for a cultural shift as the gospel in the region grows and increases.

One night this angelic Throne, who now sits in rule over Portland, came into our home unannounced. In the spirit the wall and roof at the front of our house vanished, and this heavenly prince arrived with a huge entourage of angels. I was standing in our kitchen with my wife at the time. You could literally feel their power pushing the air and changing the atmosphere into an overtly heavenly one. I began to shake uncontrollably from the intensity of the glory of God from these angels. I tried to force myself to be still, but then just had to relinquish control and allow the shaking to happen. The presence of God these angels brought with them was so intense that it got to the point where I began hollering as well as shaking. This Throne and I did not talk directly. Yet, I could hear the testimony of the righteousness of God from his silent language. He came to make an impartation and to leave an impression. Mission accomplished!

The angels really are bringing heaven to Earth. An angel later said to me, "The Throne is increasing his righteous influence daily. He is as an altar to the Lord, from his high throne. All the darkness of the region sees his high reign. It is a notice to them that says, 'We are coming.' Do not trust in the report of men. It is the report of the Lord that leads to life."

The second Throne that God established here is a Lion Throne (this Principality is not to be confused with the Lion Angel who is the Senior General of angelic forces in the area). I had been told this Throne would soon arrive. On a certain night he was in my dreams, and when I awoke during the night he was standing in a corner of my bedroom, silhouetted in a soft, glowing blue light. He needed no further introduction. He is a huge Lion, about twelve feet long, six feet high at the shoulder; and his head and mane must be four feet across. To have him here is surprisingly peaceful, but I also feel a draining of my strength. His power is intense, but it does not radiate from him, at least not in this encounter. It feels more like he pulls energy to himself, like metal to a magnet. He has not spoken a word, though the silent communication is coming

IN THE COUNSEL OF ANGELS

off him. It seems he is here because it is almost time for him to ascend to his new throne. I had wanted an update on the battle for the second Throne, and here it is.

The Lion Throne was with me all night and into the morning. I wondered why he had spent the night at our house; then I remembered my Lead Angel had said he was going to teach me to read the Thrones. This is the second godly Throne I have been with. They are shrouded with mystery. It is like looking at something that is full of energy and power, of such density and intensity that I cannot see into them. It amazes me that these majestic beings were made by our Creator; yet all their power and majesty is but a mere hint of the power and majesty of the Almighty. It is evident these Thrones are rulers; their very presence emanates authority and dominion. They have not participated in the battles for the dominions they will possess. They are the dignitaries who come to rule in righteousness after the battle is won.

The Lion Throne joined us in church that night. The scene of the angels was like a royal ceremony, full of pageantry, with the Lion Throne at center stage. Our worship leader was literally standing inside of him during the worship service, and he was visibly shaking and rocking back and forth by the time he was done leading worship.

The Lion Throne was flanked on either side by a group of four mighty angel guards. They stood on tiers or steps that descended away from the Lion. I realized he was being officially welcomed into the Portland Theater of Operations. I could tell he is a subordinate to the mighty angel Throne, who is the Senior Throne over Portland. I sensed that the rule of the godly Thrones over Portland will not be geographically

compartmentalized, like the demonic rule seemed to be. But it is in fact layered for an overlapping cumulative effect, with each Throne adding to the overall influence. Sounds just like God's love and unity to me.

I did not expect the Lion Throne back again so soon. But one night, after the others were upstairs, he showed up downstairs in our kitchen. The spirit-to-spirit communication from him told me to just go about what I had been doing, and that he was coming along when I walked my dog later that night. As promised, the Lion Throne was with me on my walk. His presence emitted his characteristics. This is a big part of the reigning function and dominion influence of a Throne. I could feel that he has no fear, and from being with him I caught the sense for a short time of what it would be like to not ever have felt fear before—such a heavenly experience. Just like a lion, he moves through his domain with kingly confidence and authority. The love of God and the peace of God in him seem to be dominant characteristics. It is a love with great confidence and strength; and a peace that projects great safety. Every aspect of the nature designed into him reflects some part of God's own attributes. I prayed for the people in the neighborhoods we walked through, that they would feel the kingdom presence of this Lion Throne and that it would settle upon their hearts and minds.

I asked the Lion, "Why are you spending time with me?"

He answered, "Kings should get used to walking with Powers." I tried to let it sink in, but after only a moment I burst out laughing. This heavenly creature said it so matter of fact. He would be the one who knows how things operate in the heavenly realms, not me.

IN THE COUNSEL OF ANGELS

He reminded me, "Don't go after a dark Throne without the Lion Angel General and his army." I must say, being with him, walking these few miles with this mighty one of God is heart-warming. And it also felt strangely normal.

On another night while on my walk, the Lion Throne and his guard showed up. His guards are eight big, powerful-looking angels perhaps ten feet tall, dressed in beautifully colored uniforms. The shafts of their spears are two inches in diameter.

So, get this picture. I am walking my dog. With me in the spirit is this huge Lion Throne. Behind us follow his eight angel guards. Overhead are my seven angel guards, and my Lead Angel is on my right. Incredible. Needless, to say, I was not alone.

I am so impressed with these amazing heavenly rulers. They are possibly some of the first beings God created. The Lion Throne is so meek and gentle; he reminds me of the Father's magnanimous gentleness, mixed with His kindness. Still, I think if this Throne were to roar he could cause an earthquake, perhaps even part the Red Sea, or fill an upper room with a mighty rushing wind.

As we walked together, we talked spirit to spirit. He had me walk out further that night, where the city limits give way to farms. I usually avoid entering this area at night because I often hear the coyote packs out there; but the peace and safety I felt being with the Throne was absolute. All of this was a taste of his reigning influence. I thanked him for helping me, and admitted I was surprised that the Lord wanted to do all this with me. He replied in his matter-of-fact manner, "We all have our part to play." There was a density and gravity to his presence, perhaps like the way we understand the stars to be densely compacted because of powerful gravitational forces. I've never been that close to a star before!

Some weeks later God's third righteous Throne for Portland presented himself to me, again with no previous notice. I was on my late-night walk with my dog through our neighborhoods. I felt in my spirit there was something walking along with me out in the street—someone very large, longer than a bus. I focused my attention on the angelic presence, and saw it was a cat, a huge black panther, perhaps forty feet long. He said nothing, but walked in the street in front of and to the right side of me. My walking route normally would take a turn at a certain location and onto a path between two houses, but this night I had earlier decided to go a different way. This panther was leading and took the different route I had intended to take.

The next morning, as I shared this experience with my wife, it hit me and I said: "This is the third Throne." He had arrived. I could feel his energy but could not pick up any communication coming off him. That could be due to my own current limitations. And he would not walk with me, but only ahead of me. I hoped there would be more contact to come, and a chance to learn more from him.

Coincidentally, I was heading over to Pastor Micah's house the following day for lunch and conversation. I wondered if the new Throne, the Black Panther, would be there. On my way over, I thought I sensed him with me. After going in the house, I sat down and Micah gave me some water. He and his son were in the kitchen, and in walked the Black Panther Throne through the front door, entryway, and ceiling. His head and

IN THE COUNSEL OF ANGELS

front quarters came in, and he stopped less than ten feet from me. I started feeling my energy drawn away and replaced with some kind of light, tingly joy.

Right then four "sheep-men" Gathering Angels walked into the room from what I learned is Micah and Danielle's room. I call them sheep-men angels because their man-like bodies are covered in thick wool. What else was I to call them? The fact that they look like sheep and are in charge of orchestrating the harvest here shows me God's sense of humor. It was then that I knew the sheep-men angels had gone home with Micah from church on Sunday and have been there ever since.

None of the angels spoke anything. During lunch I mentioned these things I was seeing. Later that night I was thinking about the Black Panther Throne and the joy I felt from him. Then it hit me. The first Throne sent by the Holy Spirit to be over Portland emits righteousness, the second Throne carries a powerful sense of peace, and now the third Throne carries joy. There it is:

> Romans 14:17, The kingdom of God is...righteousness, peace, and joy in the Holy Spirit.

God has sent Thrones with righteousness, peace, and joy to provide kingdom-rule over Portland, Oregon. It's the order in the Lord's Prayer: first,

"Your kingdom come," after that it is

"Your will be done." So, His kingdom rule has come, and now here comes "Your will be done." Yes, Lord. Let it be!

The Black Panther Throne was again with me on my walk a few nights later. He stayed well ahead of me this time, more than half a block away. Something was happening. I think it has to do with why he has come and what he is doing, but none of the angels tell me anything. They were present but had all gone silent. I thought it must be more training for me. The Lion Throne seemed comfortable walking and talking with me through his domain. Lions are social creatures. But black panthers are solitary creatures, and this Throne actually seemed as though he was focused and busy stalking something. He looked back at me several times; I think just to let me see that he was aware of me.

At morning prayer after unloading my prayers and concerns, and giving thanks, I asked my Lead Angel, "What is going on with this new Throne? The Black Panther is the third Throne, is he not?"

The angel replied, "Oh yes, he sure is. You need to ask yourself, 'What is his mission? What is he here to do?' Because he is already on his mission. What do you see?"

I said, "I see a predatory cat who is a loner. He appears to be stalking prey. What is his prey?"

We spent some time as he let me search it out. Gradually, the understanding began to come to me. The Black Panther Throne is a stalker, and he has a power to disrupt you, so that you feel an inner vulnerability. He can disrupt thoughts, feelings, beliefs, plans, conversations, circumstances, businesses, maybe governments, nature patterns, and beyond. This power to disrupt gets our attention, of course; it is something we already credit the Holy Spirit with as He works in the circumstances of our lives. That is the nature of the draining feeling when near him. He stalks his prey with his presence. But unlike a natural panther, he is not out to "kill" his prey. Joy is also imparted while he is disrupting, so the recipient of the

IN THE COUNSEL OF ANGELS

disrupting, though troubled by it, can experience comfort and be encouraged, rather than fear this process. I have experienced this disruption, or draining, from this Throne. I will simply describe it as disruption of my thoughts which definitely made me feel vulnerable, but also released joy in my spirit. It is truly a "divine contradiction." This also may explain why he usually will not let me be too close to him. And, of course, the reason this Black Panther and the Holy Spirit would disrupt someone's life is to help them see their need to "call upon the Lord."

"For whoever calls on the name of the Lord will be saved."

He will sit high over Vancouver, Washington. His reigning influence will also extend over all the Greater Portland/Vancouver Metro Area. God only knows what these Thrones of His are to do with their powers!

One morning my Lead Angel announced, "The air war for Portland is over. The three Thrones of Portland complete God's celestial government here. There is now a triangle of Thrones to consolidate God's power and dominion over the region. Think of them as air superiority.

"Now we divide the enemy on the ground, isolate them, and conquer. Our Lion Angel General and his armies will tear them up. You have been told that we are here to help. Now, believe that the numbers will increase of those who will accept the Lord. Now that the Thrones are in place, we are descending and ascending freely, (See Daniel. 10:13).

"We are setting up other staging areas for more supplies. The evangelists will come now and spread their gifts. Some of them will coordinate with the keepers of the fires (God's chosen shepherds) and will promote greater unity in the body. Pay no attention to those who grandstand, they have their reward. Just stay on mission. You have not seen anything yet."

NATIONAL ANGELIC ACTIVITY: UNDER COVER OF DARKNESS

> He made darkness His hiding place and storm clouds
> a canopy around Him.
> Psalm 18:11, BSB.

It was a day where I found myself interceding for our nation, that there would be peace and rest; something so many of us are praying into. Specifically, I was requesting disruption to the organization of anarchist rioters, and that they would fail in their objectives to cause localized and even national unrest. During these prayers and intercessions in tongues I was pulled into a vision where it was the dark of night. An angelic rider on horseback approached me. He was suited in dark armor; streaks like blue lightning flashed and swirled around every part of him and his horse; the angel's eyes were shining with white fire. He stopped his horse alongside me, looked down at me, and said, "Are you ready? Are you ready for war?"

There was no need to answer him. It was a call to intercession. He wanted me to go with him.

He said, "I am a Commander of three warrior armies." I asked, "What about my Counselors?" (I had two angel Counselors with me at the time.) "Do they come also?"

He replied, "They are your enablers. They come also."

"What will we do?"

He said, "Not all warfare is overt. We will work under cover of darkness and in the secrecy of the night. Our work is hidden from sight. We will go after enemy strongholds and tear at their foundations until they crumble. It does not matter how big the stronghold, or how big and strong the enemy looks. We will assault and destroy the foundations, and the targets will come down."

I asked him, "Do we work with anyone else?" (Meaning, another human).

His rhetorical reply required no answer. "Do I need someone else, as well?" He turned his horse and rode off into the night. I continued in prayer for a time.

Two days later while I was with one of our prophetic intercessor teams, I felt strongly to kneel and humble myself before the Lord. As I did, immediately two angels came and stood by me, then they knelt next to me. As a show of kingdom respect, they waited for me to acknowledge them. I listened as the spirit-to-spirit communication coming from them told their story. It said they were in a battle on a national front, on the east coast, led by their Commander. (Yes, the one with white fire in his eyes.) They needed reinforcements and were there asking me to make the request to God.

Upon hearing their message, at once I asked the Lord to fortify the angels' efforts and strengthen their numbers with reinforcements. Then I had this vision: I saw a fortress with hallways and rooms inside. Angels began to pour out of those rooms, flooding the hallways, and rushing to portal openings out in the courtyard. As they entered the portals, the angels flashed into light speed as they sped away. This all took some time, as it involved a very large company of angels.

I could hear tongues of angels filling the atmosphere. Orders were being given; direction and instruction for this operation. At the center of the courtyard I saw a very tall pedestal. At the top of the pedestal was a small platform on which stood a figure who was sweeping his arms from side to side. It appeared he was directing traffic by sending the angels to their various destinations. Initially I thought the figure to be an angel, just without his wings visible. However, sometime later I understood the figure was of a man; a man in prayer whom the Spirit was using to intercede for this battle. This is just one of many ways the Spirit showed me how He answers our intercessions.

DOWN COMES A MOUNTAIN

> The effective, fervent prayer of a righteous man avails much. Elijah was a man with a nature like ours, and he prayed earnestly that it would not rain; and it did not rain on the land for three years and six months. And he prayed again, and the heaven gave rain, and the earth produced its fruit. James 5:16b-18, NKJ.

I trust this story will be encouraging to many of you, especially perhaps to you who are the Lord's intercessors. I had been asking Holy Spirit for about six months when He might allow me to release the testimony of this story about answers to some of our intercessory prayers. He gave me permission in the second quarter of 2018, and I shared it at that time on my Facebook page. There are many details to this story, so I present a summary of these events here including the dates, which are important to show you the timing of the Holy Spirit, and our prayer assignments from Him. The Spirit assured me at the time that He had assigned many intercessors to take part in this battle and bring down this evil principality and stronghold, and to expose even the human element of this evil.

On July 18, 2017 the angel who is Commander of sixty legions of Special Operations angels came to me and announced that we had a new assignment. He said, "You are about to see an amazing thing."

Just then, I was drawn into the spirit realm and there was a

IN THE COUNSEL OF ANGELS

horse standing next to me. He was nudging me, using his head to brush up against my head. I responded, "What is it, boy? What is it?"

I recognized this horse. It is my horse in the spirit. I have been on him before, and he wanted me to get on him now. As I climbed onto him, I saw my clothing change into full battle gear. It was a call to fight, to advance again—a call to intercession. I began to speak in tongues.

The angel Commander said, "I will take you with us. This is part of moving in the spirit realm and being led by the Spirit. It is not necessary for people to know these things in order to operate effectively in faith. Walking in sonship and authority, and being led by the Spirit are the essentials."

I looked over at the angel and now he was sitting on a horse also. He swung his horse around in preparation to leave.

"Time to go. You are coming with us."

The angel Commander and I, and his army of 360,000 heavenly hosts now on horseback rode off like a storm of God. We accelerated to an unnatural speed. Then, as we slowed back down, it was not long before we were inside an area of deep darkness. There was a gloomy mist overhead. The atmosphere felt heavy with oppression and malice. I could tell we were approaching rulers of darkness.

Then I saw a location of four demonic Thrones shrouded in dark concealment. It looked like four large black stone sepulchers. They were dingy and seemed very old. I sensed that inside were the evil powers of witchcraft and drug abuse, false religions, gender confusion and sexual abuse, and greed and tyranny. My spirit cried out loud, "Arise O God, and let Your enemies be scattered."

This undertaking was reconnaissance for the operation I am about to tell of. New territories present new enemies, indeed. The angel Commander turned to me and said, "The enemies in this realm can easily repel those who walk in the confidence and identity of the natural man, rendering them battle-neutralized. Continue to pull together with the kingdom warriors who have prepared themselves. It is going to be quite a fight. Remind them how you want to rise to rule realms in the spirit. Some who choose to lag behind will be shocked by some of those who pay the price to march on to victory. Success in this realm and in this fight will be had by a purified faith; it is a simple faith that has been made pure. And make no mistake; this faith is your shield against the enemy's inflammatory lies. The lies will have appeal to the natural mind. Do not be seduced by them. Do not even entertain them. We have said that doubt is a potent weapon against you in this realm. And so it is in this new realm that the natural man is of necessity revealed to be in opposition to God. Yes, to be carnally minded is death, and by nature it is also in league with our demonic enemies. No kingdom warrior will be allowed at this battlefront until this allegiance to the Spirit of God is settled. For here, the warriors will operate with single-mindedness, unity, and kingdom-grade holy violence. You need only present your hearts ready for service. We will position you all in your places in the battle to produce maximum kingdom effectiveness. Remember the key:

I delight to do Your will, O God, (Psalm 40:7).

This was a call to prayer, intercession, and tongues; a call that was answered by many, many intercessors of the Lord. The Spirit of God is the One giving the call and distributing the

assignments to the hearts of His watchmen.

Two months later, on September 21, 2017, my Lead Angel approached me and said, "Are you ready to enter into a time of wonder? Faith comes through hearing. Now hear the words of God. The next Throne to be pulled down is one that is responsible for sexual abuse and sexual lust. The Commander and his army will strike hard now. Your declarations will combine with his efforts. This is a mountain. This one comes down and shakes the earth. Many prayer warriors have been summoned and are positioned in this fight. Let the hammer fall. The devils are no match for our warriors. Likewise, the devils are no match for your (plural) faith in God. The greater the victory, the more deliberate will be your thanks and praise to God. Praise and thanks to God helps release heaven to earth. This is seeing into heaven's realm and heaven's plans."

Exactly fourteen days later, on October 5, 2017, the story broke about a certain Hollywood producer being accused of serial sexual abuse of women; and from this grew the "#metoo" movement.

The biblical meaning of the number fourteen is "deliverance." A mountain stronghold was indeed pulled down, and it did shake the earth, just like the angel said it would. Blessings to all of you for your prayers and for your dedication to the Lord and His call.

> Therefore, my beloved brethren, be steadfast, immovable, always abounding in the work of the Lord, knowing that your toil is not in vain in the Lord. 1 Corinthians 15:58, NAS.

All glory to Jesus, our victorious King.

TO THE NATIONS:
IN THE HEAVENLIES OVER THAILAND

> For we do not wrestle against flesh and blood, but against principalities, against powers, against the rulers of the darkness of this age, against spiritual hosts of wickedness in the heavenly places. Ephesians 6:12, NKJ.

Towards the end of the evening service one night I was sitting on the stage riser talking with Pastor Arlan. I watched as a Battle Commander Angel rode up to us in the spirit on his very large horse. He looked down at me and said, "I need the Traveler." As he said "traveler" he turned his head and looked at Arlan and pointed at him with his chin. Then the angel turned his horse and had the right rear quarter of the horse gently brush up against Arlan's legs as the angel turned and rode away.

I shared the vision with Arlan. He said he was planning another trip to Thailand and had been looking for the Lord to provide confirmation. I realize this is one vision, yet within it I see four separate confirming elements: the angel who was sent with the message, the word "traveler," the chin-pointing, and the horse-brushing.

I went on to tell Arlan this vision of the Commander on horseback served to explain to me the meaning of a vision I had earlier that evening. I saw armies of angels walking down a number of different trails in the mountains of Southeast

IN THE COUNSEL OF ANGELS

Asia. They were pouring into the region. (I had figured this must be about Thailand.) The angels cloaked in black were walking down the mountain trails in the dark of night, and quietly heading towards the population centers. This told me there would be a surprise assault on the demonic world among the people there. God was amassing a huge number of angels to support the work of ministry and launch a major offensive. That they were arriving in stealth revealed that the evil principalities were still in rule. These cloaked angels would amass at their destinations, and at the appointed time reveal themselves and conduct the assault. I sensed this tactic would throw the enemy into great confusion.

One morning, after my prayers and intercessions were discharged, Holy Spirit had an angel take me in the spirit to be over the skies of Thailand. The skies and the heavens were dark, and there was a dark Throne ruling over the country. The dark enthronement high in the skies looked like a castle of dark clouds—sparsely lit, and very old. Winged, demon sentries would fly past my angel guide and I as they patrolled the skies. They would coast by while peering at us, but they did not confront us or oppose us. They let us pass uncontested.

Far, far down on the earth I saw the armies of the angels of God who were amassed for an assault—many tens of thousands, perhaps even hundreds of thousands of angels No doubt these were the same angels I saw in the vision filing down the mountain trails towards the cities. One angel among them who was on horseback raised a white banner. It was the signal to begin the attack against the demonic powers. One army of angels was sent to storm the powers over the seat of man's government. One army went to storm the powers over the seat of man's commerce. The third army went to assault the powers over the seat of man's religion. Three armies of God's angels were now simultaneously attacking their targets. Clearly, people had been praying. The clash of the armies of Light with the forces of darkness was so great that the darkness was forced back and had to partially release its hold on those institutions of men.

Outwardly it may appear for now like not much has changed. But this is a cultural shift occurring, being effected in the spirit realm.

> "Not by might, nor by power, but by My Spirit, says the Lord."

A little later I saw the chief satanic prince over Thailand climb part way out of his concealment in the heavenlies. He looked down at earth to see what the disturbance was about in his dominion. I began to speak to him in the name of the Lord, to oppose him with words and boldness given to me right then by Holy Spirit. The demon prince then summoned his under-rulers. Hundreds of demon lords assembled in a line to prepare for a counter assault. It looked like they were preparing to fight me and the angel who I was with. When I saw this, I became concerned. Fear attempted to grip my heart and constrict me. But I was immediately reminded of something my Lead Angel had taught me about dark Thrones. He said, "You are not to fear them." I resisted the fear and called upon the Lord. I asked Him that the hosts of heaven would intervene with overwhelming force.

The words were still on my lips when suddenly from behind me, the armies of God rushed past us at light speed and fell

IN THE COUNSEL OF ANGELS

upon the demonic lords. God's angels raged upon them with devastating power, crushing their confidence, and scattering the dark lords, sending them off in terror and mass confusion. This assault had taken the satanic prince by complete surprise. Knowing his very throne was now in jeopardy, he fully emerged from his cover to defend his rule, thus exposing his grotesque presence. To his shock and horror, not one of his under-lords returned to come to his defense. He was visibly demoralized, obviously knowing his defeat was imminent; his haughty countenance instantly deflated. The angels of the Lord then quickly came upon the dark one and seized hold of him. Wrapping him in chains, they led him away. Then a fierce and mighty, godly being descended from heaven and made his seat upon the throne over Thailand. As I watched, he leaned over his throne and spoke his first edict over his new dominion, even down to the earth, and said, "Buddha is but a man, and he is dead. Jesus is Lord of heaven and Lord of earth, and His kingdom is forever." Amen.

A CHERUB PRINCE ON HIS THRONE

> Which He worked in Christ when He raised Him from the dead and seated Him at His right hand in the heavenly places, far above all principality and power and might and dominion, and every name that is named, not only in this age but also in that which is to come.
> Ephesians 1:20-21, NKJ.

I was on my way to the prayer closet when my spirit language began to rise up from within. As I spoke it was clear this was a new-sounding tongue for me. I began to sing it, and it reminded me of what I imagine a Russian opera might sound like.

I continued until it was fully released. As this happened, I was drawn by the Holy Spirit into a heavenly realm. I found myself in a place with the most beautiful blue sky. By the Spirit I knew this location was high into the second heaven; a place purged of spiritual darkness and spiritual warfare; a realm just below the third heaven. Just then a throne on a massive stone-like platform descended into view from just above me. Seated on the throne was a majestic heavenly being. His body looked like that of a very large and powerfully muscular man. His head was that of a bull with horns. I turned towards him, and the platform and throne stopped right in front of me. This amazing creature stood up and looked right at me. I could then see that he had two sets of wings; one set large and white, and

IN THE COUNSEL OF ANGELS

the second set smaller and dark gray. This mighty cherub said to me, "Come up here."

As he spoke he also motioned with his right hand at the seat of his throne. When he did this, the throne expanded so it had room to seat two. I walked up the several steps, my eyes fixed on this being who towered over me. I sat down and so did he. I prepared myself to watch and listen.

The spirit-to-spirit communication coming off of this heavenly being told me his name, which had the meaning of "bright one." He turned his head to look down at me, and again fixed his eyes on mine. He began to speak,

"Remember that all authority comes from the Risen One. So, all other true authority has been delegated by Him, and is distributed by the Holy Spirit. Never forget that, and you will do fine. This is my throne of power, and it is now also your throne, until you are told again to come up higher. We have a commanding position here over all dark powers and principalities. You already know to only act when you are led by the Spirit and when you are sent."

I wondered how this impacted my assignment to the Portland area. He knew my question and said, "You are still assigned to Portland. But at times, we will continue to take you away to deal with dark powers elsewhere, just like what happened with Thailand. This is all part of you taking on His interests."

The visitation changed to a vision. I was in a Hall of Meeting. A holy priest was standing with a tray that had portions for the Lord's Table. A crowd of people stood in front of the priest but were facing away from him. I was in the crowd and somehow knew the priest was standing behind us. I turned around, made my way to him, and partook of the Lord's Table. Others in the crowd were also turning around and making their way to the priest. I asked, "Why doesn't everyone turn around and receive what you have for us?" The priest said, "It is only for those who listen. Those who hear will know to receive." (Jn.10:27; Rev. 3:20).

The vision of the priest ended, and I was still seated on the throne next to this mighty cherub. He said, "Do you see how walking in His authority is related to and dependent upon walking in relationship with Him and responding when He calls? The entire heavenly realm is in intimate, personal, and continual relationship with Him. To say that God is not involved with His creation is a lie from the one who sows division. (He silently gave me a Scripture, Col. 1:16-18). You Redeemed Ones have been brought back into the unity, harmony, love, and honor of His family and the heavenly order. Now let your heart and soul be purified and renewed. A king must let nothing cloud his judgment or skew his words."

He knew I had many questions, and said, "You have been told you will live in the spirit realm and work in the natural realm. You will get to know and work with many of us. You will see people transformed. You will see the earth transformed. We are enlarging your vision. Do not ever settle for less. Let the stretching continue. This is bigger than you know. Did He not say to all of you that you would do greater things than He did, if you believe? How could anyone possibly know your path? And that includes you!"

His wisdom entered my ear like water to a thirsty man. His manner was so regal, conveying to me great honor and respect. Also, there is an extraordinary gentleness to this magnificent

IN THE COUNSEL OF ANGELS

heavenly being. As the visitation ended, I caught a glimpse of his head as he seemed to turn it, switching from a bull to a lion.

Some weeks later, I had been speaking in tongues most of the day while I went about my activities. Late afternoon and on into the evening, the urgency to pray in tongues was especially compelling. A missions team had traveled with Pastor Micah to Mazatlan, Mexico, yet I was given no real understanding of what the intercession was about. I went on my walk late that night and

> "YOU WILL SEE PEOPLE TRANSFORMED. YOU WILL SEE THE EARTH TRANSFORMED. WE ARE ENLARGING YOUR VISION. DO NOT EVER SETTLE FOR LESS. LET THE STRETCHING CONTINUE. THIS IS BIGGER THAN YOU KNOW. DID HE NOT SAY TO ALL OF YOU THAT YOU WOULD DO GREATER THINGS THAN HE DID, IF YOU BELIEVE?"

continued praying in tongues. During my walk I was ushered into the presence of that mighty cherub on his throne. As I approached, I noticed he was standing up in front of his throne. Holy Spirit spoke in my heart that this being was standing as a show of heavenly respect for me, a son of God, a king, and a priest. I was so happy to be able to meet with him again.

I said, "All that praying today was working with you, wasn't it?"

He said, "Yes".

I asked if I could understand how this praying worked with the angels in the spiritual warfare. But he replied, "It is better to stand, than to understand." His silent language reassured me that the understanding would come, in time. But as always

in the kingdom, the learning is in the doing, and the doing is by faith. I felt the approval from him, and his kingdom-joy of working with me; a joy which I shared towards him as well.

DEMYSTIFYING THE SPIRIT REALM

THE UNSEEN IS THE ETERNAL

> While we do not look at the things which are seen, but at the things which are not seen. For the things which are seen are temporary, but the things which are not seen are eternal.
> 2 Corinthians 4:18, NKJ.

During one visit the Lord Jesus said to me, "I want you to help demystify the spirit realm for the people." So far, He has chosen to prepare me in this assignment by having the Holy Spirit and His angels take me with them into the unseen spirit realm so I can see and experience it for myself. His Word encourages all of us to pay attention to heavenly things,

> "Set your minds on things that are above (heavenly things), not on things that are on earth."
> Colossians 3:2, ESV.

Some believers think, "Oh, that spiritual stuff, it's not for me. I'm not like that." Dear one, if you are alive in Jesus Christ, you are born of heaven. God's Word is food for your spirit man. Ask the Lord to help you put aside your earthly identity and take on the new man who is alive with Jesus in the

IN THE COUNSEL OF ANGELS

spirit realm. You do not have to go anywhere or do anything to get there. The nature of this new man is spoken of lavishly in God's Word. By your faith it is the reality of who you are made to be in Him. That is why we seek to walk in the Spirit.

> If we live by the Spirit, let us also walk by the Spirit.
> Galatians 5:25, NAS.

God is Spirit. He is invisible and He lives in an invisible realm. Look around you. Everything your eyes can see is temporary; everything! The natural universe and all its vast expanse will one day come to an end. It will not end due to some theorized cataclysmic chain of natural events. God will end it, for He has said so. The things which are seen are only temporary, while those things which are not seen are eternal. This temporary world of ours, and the universe itself, exists inside the infinite, eternal God and His invisible spirit realm. God surrounds and permeates our natural realm of time and space. It takes no effort at all for Him to simply reach in and impact our natural world, and that includes sending His angels to minister, for He is not far from us at all. This is why Paul could say,

> "So that they should seek the Lord, in the hope that they might grope for Him and find Him, though He is not far from each one of us; for in Him we live and move and have our being, as also some of your own poets have said, 'For we are also His offspring.'"
> Acts 17:27-28, NKJ.

God is far closer and more intimately in touch with His creation than many people have considered or experienced. Can you think of anyone other than God who knows how many hairs are on your head? And even with all the cameras present in our over-surveilled world, does anyone other than God know when each and every sparrow falls to the ground in death? The eyes of the Lord are everywhere, for He watches over us all.

The Creator spoke His words from the unseen realm and created all the visible things.

> By faith we understand that the worlds were prepared by the word of God, so that what is seen was not made out of things which are visible. Hebrews 11:3, NAS.

And so, His unseen spirit realm is preeminent over our natural universe that is passing away. Today, when God speaks, it still comes from the unseen, spirit realm. (When the angels talk to me in reference to their unseen realm, they most often used the term "spirit realm." That is why I also use that term.)

The entire Bible, the Word of God, was spoken from the spirit realm and recorded as Holy Spirit moved upon men.

> Every Scripture is God-breathed and profitable for instruction, for conviction, for correction, and for training in righteousness. 2 Timothy 3:16.

The Spirit of God is always encouraging us to walk by faith in the promises God gives. In other words, He wants us to believe the eternal words that He has spoken to us from the spirit realm. We have access to the spirit realm through faith in Jesus Christ. All faith transactions that we conduct with God occur in the spirit realm. God has matched His words, which are from the spirit realm, to our new man in Christ who is also alive in the spirit realm, even while we live on the earth in these natural bodies of flesh. Reading the Bible is more than just a good idea. The reality is that His Word is food for our spirits.

> But he answered, "It is written, Man shall not live by bread alone, but by every word that comes from the mouth of God." Matthew 4:4, ESV.

DOMINION IS THE CHILDREN'S BREAD

> For we do not wrestle against flesh and blood, but against principalities, against powers, against the rulers of the darkness of this age, against spiritual hosts of wickedness in the heavenly places.
> Ephesians 6:12.

When we wrestle with the unseen forces of darkness it is for the purpose of victory and dominion. It is through faith in the name of Jesus and by His blood that we overcome. Let's define a couple of terms being used here. "Realms" are areas or spheres of influence. "Dominions" are realms or areas where authority and supremacy have been secured. This is not to be confused with the word "dominions" in the Bible that is a reference to spirit beings.

My Lead Angel offered some instruction. He said, "I am going to teach you about realms and dominions. Constantly, there are sons and daughters who are brought by the Spirit into realms and dominions, for you are all children of the Spirit. This happens most frequently while they are in prayer, but also in visions and dreams. Some understand where the access point is, and can return to the power. But far too many still experience it as if they have stumbled into it; but they have no real clarity how to return. Many unwittingly even attempt to return by

IN THE COUNSEL OF ANGELS

means of the natural man. Needlessly they will construct a reasoned formula hoping to recreate the conditions when they previously experienced access, only to fail. This happens to individuals, and it has even taken down whole moves of God that left off following the Spirit and sought to pursue religious practices and principles that in themselves contain no life. The natural man cannot transcend the natural realm; neither can he operate by faith. You are children of the Spirit. Your new man is born of the Spirit and is made to operate in faith. Faith is an active moving in the spirit realm. Only while operating in the identity of your new man and by faith can you enter the operations in the spirit realm. This must become clear to the sons and daughters. You are all to grow and become very effective spiritual warriors and overcomers in your stations. And it has been decreed that it will become a life priority and a standard within the body unity.

"There are levels and layers, realms, spheres, and dominions in the spirit realm. Many, many doors are meant to be accessed. Some doors will be open. Some doors will be closed but unlocked. Some locked doors are intended to be unlocked and then accessed. We will talk another time about doors that must be closed and locked, and doors that must remain locked. This now is about loosing and releasing. This is about kingdom keys. This is a time of accelerated growth and we want you to continue to keep it up for the sake of your training and release. Intimacy with Him remains the pursuit, with the rooting and grounding in love always the goal. For sons and daughters, your access to the spirit realm is by faith, and through the Spirit and in the Spirit."

"For this is war. You are His love-warriors, overcoming evil with the power of good from the Holy Spirit. Notice I did not say that the power of good was to come from your natural man. All good works are best rooted in the power of the Spirit. There will be many in that day who say, 'Lord, we did all these great things in your name.' But for some, the works they did were done apart from Him being involved.

"My sword now brings clarity to the matter, by dividing and separating: the light from the darkness, the heavenly from the earthly, the spiritual from the natural, fruitfulness from dead works, God's purposes from man's purposes, acting in concert with God versus acting alone and saying it is His work. Judge which is better: Acting from the reasoning and intent of the natural man, and then dressing it up on the outside to make it appear as if it is of the Spirit; or hearing the Great Shepherd's voice and then following the leading of the Spirit to perform His will and do His works? Realms in the spirit are areas of influence. Dominion in these realms is an exercising of the authority the Spirit has delegated and released. Dominion-authority is achieved after faith is tried, and after the enemies in the realm are overcome. Intercessory prayer can cause entry into a realm and be an influence there. The same is true of a gift of the Spirit (I Corinthians 12: 1-11), a motivation gift (Romans 12: 3-8), and a ministry office (Ephesians 4: 11-13).

> INTIMACY WITH HIM REMAINS THE PURSUIT, WITH THE ROOTING AND GROUNDING IN LOVE ALWAYS THE GOAL. FOR SONS AND DAUGHTERS, YOUR ACCESS TO THE SPIRIT REALM IS BY FAITH, AND THROUGH THE SPIRIT AND IN THE SPIRIT."

There are many ways for you to operate in the spirit realm, and every one of them must be done so by active faith."

The angel stopped so I could ponder his words and let the lesson sink in. I am glad he did, because he sure said a mouthful, and my spirit was stuffed full at the time! He let me know this was but a preamble to what he intends to show me. He introduced his topic and would proceed with it in its order and time.

The next night on my walk, my Lead Angel appeared in the spirit and continued sharing his understanding

"Learn of realms in the spirit world and how to have dominion over them. And learn of dominions that are apportioned and how to match them with the realms where they will govern. Realms will often have doors or gates, which may also need keys. The only reason for a son or daughter to go through a door or a gate is to gain mastery over the realm being entered. This is kingdom rule. You are thinking that Christ already gave all keys and all authority to His church. This is true; but there is a growing that happens. Do you expect a child to fly a jet airplane? No, you may first have them master walking; later a bicycle, a car, and so on. Head-knowledge of positional biblical truths has not served to mature the Church throughout its history. Kingdom authority is exercised from the spirit-man, the hidden man of the heart; this is where the growth takes place. In the inner man is where revelation instructs; and where discernment, wisdom, and power operate. There is a barrier and a divide here that causes many to stumble, and to never advance beyond it. Placing one's faith and trust in the word of the Lord and following His lead will move one through the natural man's barrier of unbelief, and forward into the spirit realm, where

all kingdom-transactions occur. You believe what He says, and then you act on it. Having to learn by doing is one of our safeguards against unlawful entry. You must be invited in by faith in a word from God. In the atmosphere of righteousness, peace, and joy is where you find the Spirit at work. Entering a new realm is spiritual growth. Pay attention and read the realms for yourself, and for others when useful. Illuminate the paths. Help people to read what they are sensing, and to interpret what it means. You are brought to the doors of realms that you might enter there. Then, when you have secured dominion and have the mastery, these realms are brought to you. The centurion recognized Jesus' dominion over sickness. He knew that his servant's need would be met because it was within a realm where Christ had already demonstrated dominion. Then that need was brought to Jesus by faith—great faith.

"All new realms are entered by faith and with faith. This is why the current upgrade of the Spirit includes an increase of faith: so you all can enter the new realms of influence He has for you, and learn to exercise His kingdom authority and dominion in these realms. For no one is to be left behind. This is all part of a master class and master teaching. It is accessible to those who will first rule their own souls. The refining fire continues to burn on the body. The invitation to come boldly to Him remains a steady call that can be heard. When a lesson is learned, authority is given and activation is released. Then another lesson comes. The lessons will come now as fast as you each allow. The acceleration in the spirit you experience is because our spirit realm operates at the faster pace of the life of God, while your natural realm is passing away. These are kingdom-strides and we are here to help you. Religious

IN THE COUNSEL OF ANGELS

practice is not of faith, nor of the kingdom, but is of the world. The cry of religious practice is, 'There must be limits!' The blindness of the natural man! It is a drive that seeks to quench a thing and thereby control it. This is the way of the natural man. There is no life in it, but only man's righteousness which he will wear as a badge of self-achievement. But the way of faith leads to abundant life from the kingdom of heaven. It yields growth, openness, dependency on Him, and kingdom-fruitfulness with joy.

"To walk in kingdom authority within a realm, you must by faith actually enter that realm. The enemies are confronted, and then the growing begins. When the enemies are defeated, then the mastery comes. Then the son and the daughter possess a level of kingdom authority and its inheritance. And we repeat it all again. Run after the kingdom. Run after your assignment. You run to Him. Run to know Him. And when you are running, your sword is out in front. Your running is to be the running by faith. The word of faith is in your heart, and your mouth, and your hand. The kingdom warriors are commited to growth: growth in faith, wisdom, understanding, knowledge, discernment, mercy, love, grace, and so on. This is the posture of the kingdom warrior. These are among the things that are from above. It is the workings in the unseen realm where you are alive unto God. It is who you are.

"You are all running to the battle. And the battle is not yours, but the Lord's. Do not allow your cares to distract you from minding your assignment. We must keep the coming of the kingdom moving along at its pace, and you have your part to play. Know the times and understand the seasons. This is the time for greater faith. Be open to the unusual, the unexpected, and the unannounced. Now, imagine you come to a gate for a realm, knowing that victory there leads to kingdom-multiplication. Greater faith is your key of entry. What would happen there? What would it look like in your world? It would shake human culture there to its foundations. It would turn the world around you upside-down. For nothing will be impossible to the one who believes.

"The wailing hearts of the intercessors and the battle cries of the advancing warriors will mix with the ground-swell of praise and thanksgiving from the people to help call it forward. The Father is prepared to release it. It is His response to the calls from His children that enters into His ears. Do you see why you are instructed to set your affections on the things above? Do you see why your salvation is closer now than when you first believed? This is the urgency of seeking His kingdom first. Fan the flames. Let the fires burn. This combines to release powerful kingdom joy and thanks. Do you see why we work to burn away the chaff and stubble from you before the young ones arrive? They will imitate the fervency of your spirits in Christ.

"Kingdom keys are meant to be used. They are of little value if not put to use when needed. You can show another how to use their keys. You can alert their attention to keys they have and help them unlock the door, the door to the realm they are appointed to enter. Willing warriors will appreciate the push in the right direction.

"Remember, keys are for doors. Doors open to realms. Realms are for dominion. And dominion is the children's' bread, your kingdom inheritance. Members in the body are moving in obedience into realms, that they might learn dominion

IN THE COUNSEL OF ANGELS

there. Many are feeling just as disoriented as you are in your assignment. Comfort and encourage His people. You are all the planting of the Lord. When you enter a new realm in the spirit, know from the very first that it is intended for you to become a ruler over that realm. That is the reason you have entered that realm. When you have grown and have the mastery there, then we can take you to another realm for the same purpose. You can re-enter a realm where you have dominion at a moment's notice, when the need arises. This is kingdom authority and part of growing and moving in the spirit realm and being led by the Spirit. It is not necessary for people to know these things I tell you in order for them to operate in them. Walking in sonship and authority, and being led by the Spirit are the essentials here. But we want to show these workings to you so you can track us and read our work. This is part of the celestial order.

"Jesus is King of every realm, in heaven and in earth. He has all the keys. Each new realm you enter is lavishly decorated with the glorious gospel of Christ. Look for it. And why would it not be that way? For in the throne room of God itself, the Lamb of God is the centerpiece. The Lamb is the love of God expressed. You can all live forever because of the Lamb. All other blessings flow out of what the Lamb has accomplished. Do you see now how my sword speaks? (The angel was referring to the words of his mouth.) The intercessors will pick up on these things the quickest, for they are the ones most used to navigating the spirit realm. This includes the shepherds, for they too are intercessors. As you all accumulate access to new realms, many in the body will sense the newness as kingdom-substance and life, and this will be an ongoing attractant and encouragement to many. This has already been in play for some time, but now its influence will intensify, spread, and increase. He gives grace and glory. No good thing will He withhold from those who walk uprightly."

UNITY AND FELLOWSHIP OF THE SPIRIT

> Then His (Jesus) mother and His brothers arrived, and standing outside they sent word to Him and called Him. A crowd was sitting around Him, and they said to Him, "Behold, Your mother and Your brothers are outside looking for You." Answering them, He said, "Who are My mother and My brothers?" Looking about at those who were sitting around Him, He said, "Behold My mother and My brothers! For whoever does the will of God, he is My brother and sister and mother."
> Mark 3:31-35, BSB.

One day I was in the spirit and in the company of an enthroned cherub prince (whom I mentioned in Chapter 2). During this visit he and I touched on the topic of unity of the Spirit. He had just given his approval that my wife and I had obeyed the Spirit's leading to pray about certain things this particular day. I asked him, "Should she and I then increase our praying together?"

That could seem like a fair question; honestly, I reasoned that if some prayer had been good, then maybe more prayer would be better. But alas, God does not need my bright ideas.

This magnificent heavenly being, knowing my thoughts and the motives of my heart, used the opportunity to make clear the discernment between good human intentions (which originates of earth and flesh), and being led by the Holy Spirit (which originates from heaven). He spoke like a wise counselor full of kindness

"Unity of the Spirit does not come about from doing things together. The unity of the Spirit can work among you when each person goes to the cross in their own life as a daily practice of yielding to His will. The dying to self-will and then the resurrection into doing His will is what promotes the unity of the Spirit among the members of the body. Then you preserve that unity by showing honor and preferring one another. Natural human thinking says that doing things together is unity. But in the kingdom, unity is not an activity; it is a matter of the heart, and a matter of the first degree. Seek first the kingdom of God and His righteousness. First you are to find communion with Him because of the work of the cross you allow upon your heart daily. Then, you find unity and fellowship with those who are also allowing the same working of the Spirit in their lives. Men will try to simulate and imitate this work, in order to retain control of their life. But this is a work of the Spirit and not of the flesh, and you will know to discern the difference in the spirit."

> "UNITY OF THE SPIRIT DOES NOT COME ABOUT FROM DOING THINGS TOGETHER. THE UNITY OF THE SPIRIT CAN WORK AMONG YOU WHEN EACH PERSON GOES TO THE CROSS IN THEIR OWN LIFE AS A DAILY PRACTICE OF YIELDING TO HIS WILL."

I wish you could have heard and felt the honor and dignity expressed to me as this heavenly being issued his counsel and

IN THE COUNSEL OF ANGELS

wisdom. His words captured my heart with the sweet savor of truth. A few moments later, he was gone; but the impact from his words remains.

In the above passage from Mark 3, we see Jesus giving a teaching about the realm in which kingdom relationships operate. Unity of the Spirit and fellowship of the Spirit is established by accessing and doing the will of God. Jesus was not shunning His biological family or minimizing that reality. Later, while on the cross, Jesus displayed His love and care for His mother when He spoke to her and John, telling them they were now mother and son and indicating that they were to look after one another. Unity of the Spirit and fellowship of the Spirit are not founded on a human organizational level. The things of the Spirit originate from the spirit realm. They do not originate from earth or from things that are of the earth. They are not founded on a human social level. They are not founded on human bloodlines. Kingdom-relationships, and therefore fellowship and unity of the Spirit, are founded on the level of doing the will of God. We still have the ability to speak with and interact with anyone, regardless of where they are in their life and their relationship with the Lord. But I am not referring here to mere communication with our fellow human beings. Kingdom-fellowship with one another is a relationship in the spirit realm. Doing the will of God is the unifying bond that brings us into this "koinonia" fellowship. Doing the will of God also gives true meaning and order to our human social and human family relationships.

"For whoever does the will of God, he is My brother and sister and mother."

This unity is a condition of the heart; it is accessed through transformation by the renewal of the mind, which then enables you to prove the will of God (see Rom 12:1-2.). Walking in the will of God, which includes walking in His light, provides access to the fellowship of the Spirit with one another.

> But if we walk in the light as He is in the light, we have fellowship with one another, and the blood of Jesus His Son cleanses us from all sin. 1 John 1:7, BSB.

Jesus made it plain and clear what a high priority it is to Him that we seek to know and come to do His will.

REBUKED BY AN ANGEL

> Zacharias said to the angel, "How will I know this for certain? For I am an old man and my wife is advanced in years." The angel answered and said to him, "I am Gabriel, who stands in the presence of God, and I have been sent to speak to you and to bring you this good news. And behold, you shall be silent and unable to speak until the day when these things take place, because you did not believe my words, which will be fulfilled in their proper time."
> From Luke 1: 18-20, NAS.

In the encounter between the angel Gabriel and Zechariah the priest, we see Zechariah's response of unbelief towards what the angel said to him. It stands as an example to us of how NOT to respond to God and His angels who bring His message. And we see the angel issuing his judgment against Zechariah.

Angels are truth-tellers. Depending on the need of the occasion, they can be gentle and subtle, or starkly direct and authoritative. Fortunately for me, offended angels do not carry grudges or hold things against us. In my experience they get things out in the open, and deal with them right then and there, just like Gabriel did with Zechariah. I can personally assure you that an angel can cause the fear of the Lord to instantly come upon you.

The following rebukes were issued to me by my Lead Angel. I admit I needed the attitude adjustments. Since part of my ministry is to confront unbelief, it makes perfect sense for the Holy Spirit to help me get from my own attitudes of unbelief. These lessons were very unpleasant at the time, although I do laugh about them a bit now though.

> And have you forgotten the exhortation that addresses you as sons? 'My son, do not regard lightly the discipline of the Lord, nor be weary when reproved by him. For the Lord disciplines the one He loves, and chastises every son whom He receives." Heb.12:5-6, NAS. And, "We are ready to punish all disobedience, whenever your obedience is complete.
> 2 Cor.10:6, NAS.

While in prayer on a certain day, the sweet peace of His presence descended on me and I was led through some prayers. My Lead Angel surprised me when he said, "Why should I tell you more, if you are not going to believe me?" That is all he said at the time, and then he left. Talk about a bad start to your day! The context was that he had been patiently leading me to trust what he said as he gave understanding to me about the Lord's assignment. And of course, he was aware of the inner battle I faced as my doubts fought against the word of the Lord being relayed through him. I know that God is intensely focused on relentlessly removing any vestige of doubt or unbelief in me.

I understood that the angel intended me to doubt my doubts, not doubt what he said.

Make no mistake, angels sent to you already know you. There is nothing in you hidden from their sight. They deal

IN THE COUNSEL OF ANGELS

in truth and yes, they have mercy and grace. Understand that to be chastened by the Lord means He wants us to share in His holiness (see Hebrews 12:7-11). This is a great trade He makes with us. I want to feel the new wine stretching the new wineskin!

This next rebuke was for pride. It was not for the boasting kind of pride, but the kind that diminished what the angel said as seeming unimportant. I had spent some time in prayer and intercession. My Lead Angel spoke, "Time to forget the things that are behind, the deficits of the past. You are brought to new riches, fresh oil, and new life. Step into it with complete confidence and abandon. We love the new man. We work with the new man. We do not and cannot work with the old man. Your (plural) prayers will help the fire of His presence to spread. Angelic encounters will be reported now with greater frequency. People will be touched by the glory of God through us. I told you, we are working together with you (plural). Cast down strongholds, cast out demons, heal the sick, raise the dead, open blind eyes, open deaf ears, and loose mute tongues. We work kingdom works with you."

I said to the angel, "No offense, but much of what you are saying here sounds kind of generic. Can you tell me more specific things?"

The angel discerned my motive and quickly countered with, "Your pride belongs on the cross. Do it immediately and we will not miss a step together."

In his judgment he gave me a choice. That's mercy. So, I thought, what to do? Miss a step with the angel (and the Holy Spirit) and come under judgment, or repent now, be free of it, and remain in his good graces. I instantly told him, "I repent for pride and for wanting to hear things beyond what you choose to share. Lord Jesus, may your blood cleanse me of this sin. Not my will, but Yours be done."

Honestly, I think I was a little tired at the time. My mind was sluggish, and I missed his point. I let down my guard and got careless with my words: open mouth, insert foot. As I am learning, what an angel has to say is the very thing that needs to be said at that moment; and therefore, it is the very thing I am supposed to listen to and heed.

The angel then coached me, "You need to appreciate the position you are in; where we have placed you. A good number of our operations here also include our interactions with you. Learn your place. It is substantial. Turn your questions towards knowing your role with us. Focus!" I told him I was sorry and that I would do my best.

I was out on my walk with my dog late one night, and I sensed the presence of angels. My guard of seven angels was with me, circling overhead. My Lead Angel was there, so I asked him to tell me something. He reminded me how he told me that he would also come to me in signs in the earth and sky, and that we would speak often.

There was a breeze blowing as he said, "I will now also come to you in the wind. Whenever there is a wind and wherever you are, I will be there in the wind."

I asked, "What should I know about? Can I understand more of God's plan for Portland?" (Did you notice right there how I just casually changed subjects on the angel; bad idea!) He huffed at me.

"Do you think God has a plan for the Portland area?" (I could feel the anger rising up in his words.) "Do you think

IN THE COUNSEL OF ANGELS

it can be revealed to a man?" (I had really set him off this time. "Yikes, I'm in trouble again. Lord, help.") This time his delivery was sharp and his tone was stern.

"No matter how much revelation you are given, you will still have to walk by faith. Revelation knowledge does not eliminate the need for faith. Rather, it illuminates the path that is to be walked on by faith. The body is to look for us during all the different times and places of meeting. Welcome us also, as you welcome the Spirit, for we work His will among you. You do not pray to us, but you ask the Spirit to bring the kingdom among you. We are here to shower you with the blessings of the kingdom."

Did you see the angel's conversational flow? He issued his rebuke to me and was done with it. No lingering frustration or telling me how I had inconvenienced him. Once he saw I repented he got right back on topic, on his mission. Part of learning the angels' ways has been to come to understand how to speak with them, (and how not to speak to them) and how to really tune in to listen for what they are revealing.

HAWK ANGEL

LION ANGEL GENERAL

CONTACT FROM HEAVEN

"All the facial features of a natural lion,
but his bright green eyes shine with a deep
heavenly intelligence."
Page 79

BLACK PANTHER THRONE (PRINCE)

A REIGN OF INFLUENCE

"Unlike a natural panther, he is not out to kill his prey. He releases joy even as he disrupts our natural thoughts."
Pages 118-119

THE SPIRIT REALM NEVER SLEEPS...

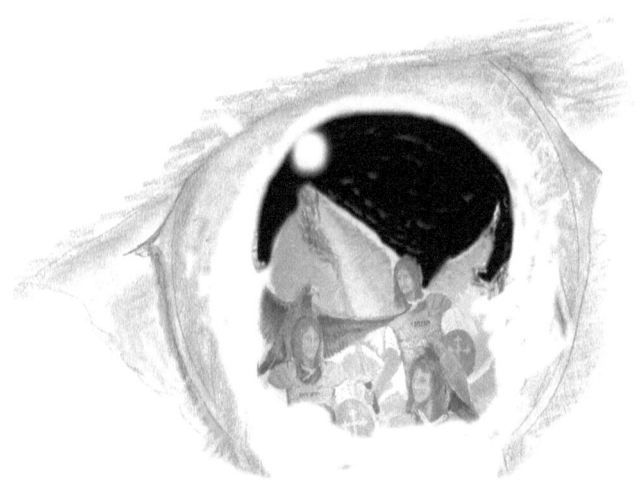

"The angels appointed to me have come as counselors..."
Page 56

HE IS AT THE DOOR

BECOME MY INTERCESSOR

"Behold, I stand at the door and knock. If anyone hears My voice and opens the door, I will come in to him and dine with him, and he with Me."
Revelation 3:20, NKJ

This section highlights the story of my personal re-awakening into the present-tense fellowship with the living God. God never made me feel shame for having to pass through the testing in the wilderness. I was still His son, enduring His disciplining. Like the father in Jesus' story of the Two Brothers (we call it the "Prodigal son"), God welcomed me into His presence with open arms of love and acceptance; there is a ring, a robe, and a feast with the celebration of joy as the Father welcomes us into the maturity of sonship, being in the Father's house, and being about the Father's business!

One morning a few years back, while already in prayer, the Holy Spirit said to me, "I want you to become My intercessor." I knew how to pray, and I knew what intercession was, so I thought. But the Holy Spirit is not the least bit impressed with our experience, nor does He need our advice. The Spirit caused me to recognize that within those seven words, He had something fresh and new in mind for me.

Thankfully His wisdom also came with the revelation. My approach was to be a simple one. My obedience was to be unquestioning. I was to jettison any of my pre-conceived notions that sought to interfere with His way. I was to let Him lead entirely; for He was about to teach me fresh new ways of His kingdom. The measure of God's grace on me must have been very great, because I ended up doing it exactly the way He wanted. "To obey is better than sacrifice." Obey Him and He shows you more, abundantly more; beyond all we could ask or even think.

COME TO THE QUIET

"If my people who are called by my name humble themselves, and pray and seek my face and turn from their wicked ways, then I will hear from heaven and will forgive their sin and heal their land."
2 Chronicles 7:14, ESV.

This verse is so often cited as a key to cultural awakening; yet it is also a key to a personal awakening. It was the Holy Spirit who first directed me to this Scripture and showed me to apply it on a personal level, to myself. Personal awakening to God must precede participation in a cultural awakening.

My new focus of becoming one of His intercessors was accompanied by the understanding the Holy Spirit was to lead, and I was to do nothing without His leading. Each time I hit the prayer closet I would completely surrender the time, the agenda, and my faculties to Him. My Bible was ready, and pencil and notebook were at hand; I was set for listening. The Spirit and I would pour over the Scriptures together as He released His glorious illumination to me. I never knew what was coming next, or what He had planned for me. He was leading, and I was following. Holy Spirit termed this effort as "Come to the Quiet"; such an appealing and pleasant-sounding invitation! He wanted His ideas and plans for me to become my only motivating interest; none of my preconceived

notions of what I thought it meant to serve God were to be pulled from the archives of my knowledge or my years of experience. That included a letting go of all that I thought He had promised so He could rearrange my life the way any way He wanted to, with no objection or hesitation from me. Do you remember how God required father Abraham to trust Him even when He told him to offer-up Isaac, the embodiment of God's promise? Abraham's faith passed through God's crucible of circumstance. By grace, we are made to have like-faith with Abraham (Romans 4:16-18).

This "Come to the quiet" to be with Him became the highest goal in my life. Day after day for many months I worked with Him diligently to seek, listen, and learn. I later recognized that this process was also retraining my over-active mind; renewing it and disciplining it on how to truly be still before Him. The severe testing I had been through uniquely prepared my disposition: I was desperate for the Living God to be real in my life. I was no longer bound by the misguided obligations of religious duty; no longer unresponsive, or as dull of hearing towards Him. Instead, there was eagerness, anticipation, and faith! Yes, there was a heart-felt willingness to believe Him. He now held my reins, because I handed them over to Him. He had been patiently coaxing me through the years to do that very thing. It was as if there came a heavenly reset of our "potter and clay" relationship that was allowing Him and me to flow with one another in a way my heart had only dreamed of. I understood that to walk in this place would require living on a level of faith and listening to Him that I had previously touched on but never consistently walked in. In short, His invitation was one of renewed total surrender.

There was the clear sense that I could not reach this high mark without the Spirit's help. God also gave glimpses of things He was calling me to that were entirely impossible to achieve on my own. (Sound familiar?) And He gave me clear assurance of His will and His direction for my life.

There is strong encouragement when the heart is assured by Him through the knowledge of His will (see Romans 12:1-2). "Come to the Quiet" then, is the place of rest that is by faith (see Hebrews 4).

On our part, He tells us to, "Draw near to God"; then, on God's part, "He will draw near to you" James 4:8a. How can we who believe in Jesus live our lives any other way? Jesus said,

> "My sheep hear my voice, and I know them, and they follow me." John 10:27.

Did Jesus mean this "hearing of His voice" literally or not? Or is God a mute, like the idols of wood, stone, and concrete that some people worship? If He is not to be taken literally, then why would He say such a thing? There is only one possible answer. He said it because He means it! Have you ever stilled yourself before God and waited until He spoke to you? Have you come to Him and remained there, so you can hear from Him; to hear from Him and His Holy Spirit in your spirit, whether audibly, through His Word, or any other way He chooses? You young people should test what you think you hear from the Lord by sharing it with those who are older; individuals who already fellowship with one another on this level, and who sharpen each other's hearing and discernment. Then, when you know you hear Him, you

IN THE COUNSEL OF ANGELS

obey what He has said. It involves a combination of hunger, desperation, discernment, faith, and dogged determination. Hear Him when He makes Himself known, and then perhaps most important for us, do that very thing. Then, the next time you come to our Father you can report to Him that you have carried out His wishes, and that you are now ready for more. The ways of the Spirit, the ways of faith, the ways of the kingdom are so wonderful and amazing!

I shudder to think that anyone might consider this "Come to the Quiet" as another prayer technique. It is in fact the raw reality of waiting upon Him who is the Living God. It is coming to Jesus, who is the "door" (John 10:9).

Here is what I do. Once I have begun, I make no sound at all and wait to hear His still small voice, and anything He might say or want to show me. This could take a moment, a minute, or hours, especially if you are new to this. For those who find this pursuit to be new, remember: come in faith. God rewards faith (Hebrews 11:6).

When I first began this practice there were times when I stilled myself for two or three hours, or even longer, and waited to hear Him. Does that sound excessive, even unreasonable and unrealistic? I would agree. But if I am going to follow Jesus, I want to hear and experientially know His voice. It is not enough for me to know "about" Him. I must know HIM; and therefore, I must hear Him. Fortunately for us, the desire of His heart has always been to reveal Himself to us, His children. There's that divine alignment; our coming into agreement with the will of God. I will wait for Him until He shows up!

Make no mistake; this was surrendering to the fire of

God and staying there as He took me on a guided tour of searching and purging the motives of my heart and soul.

> "The spirit of man is the lamp of the Lord, searching all the innermost parts of his being." Proverbs 20:27.

> "Every branch in Me that does not bear fruit, He takes away; and every branch that bears fruit, He prunes it so that it may bear more fruit." John 15:2, NAS.

Holy Spirit loves to sort through and prioritize our "stuff" with us. I now live and abide in His fire, and He is free to search me and change me whenever and however He chooses. At first, you may need a thorough housecleaning. This is not for the half-hearted or the insincere. This reset will likely take months; it certainly did for me. This is the commitment; there is no turning back, but only following the Holy Spirit's lead. I am talking about allowing the holy fire of God to select and choose to burn up everything that it wants to, anything He chooses. He gets to target and remove anything He considers to be unnecessary and unimportant in my life. (See John 15:1-8.) If you want to prove to your own heart that you trust Him, then

> IF I AM GOING TO FOLLOW JESUS, I WANT TO HEAR AND EXPERIENTIALLY KNOW HIS VOICE. IT IS NOT ENOUGH FOR ME TO KNOW "ABOUT" HIM. I MUST KNOW HIM; AND THEREFORE, I MUST HEAR HIM. FORTUNATELY FOR US, THE DESIRE OF HIS HEART HAS ALWAYS BEEN TO REVEAL HIMSELF TO US.

IN THE COUNSEL OF ANGELS

walk through His fire with Him. It will burn up the garbage, but I can assure you He will also choose to burn up some things which you value as precious. The test is on! Who will you make lord—yourself or Him?

We are still talking about seeking Him and being in His Presence. There have been times when seeking Him that I have fallen asleep in His presence without hearing Him. Such sweet slumber! Other times, I simply did not hear Him, for whatever reason. But I kept coming back. I just kept knocking, like Jesus tells us to, until the door is opened.

One day a friend, who has been a missionary for many years, told me that he wanted more of God; he wanted to be closer to Him. I felt a strong but gentle leading of the Spirit to invite him to "Come to the Quiet" during his devotions, so we talked about it. The following week he told me he had done this. He said he was shocked to discover the "wound-up" condition of his mind. It had taken him over an hour just to quiet his busy mind. That's what I discovered too.

How can we possibly expect to hear God if we are in such a wound-up, over-stimulated, and distracted mental and emotional state? How can we ever feel what His heart feels when we are saturated with earthly activities and cares, and are already fully preoccupied? Many Christians are so busy with activities, and dealing with the schedules, demands, and stresses of life that they have no idea what it is to still their souls before God and actually listen for Him. This is, at its root, an issue of priorities. Jesus laid it out to us: *"Seek first the Kingdom of God and His righteousness,"* and

"...those who hunger and thirst after righteousness are blessed because they will be filled." The truth is, of course, that He is the One who has been seeking us all along.

THE SECRET PLACE OF ABIDING

He that dwells in the secret place of the most High, shall abide under the shadow of the Almighty.
Psalm 91:1.

"Abide in Me, and I in you. As the branch cannot bear fruit of itself unless it abides in the vine, so neither can you unless you abide in Me." John 15:4

"Be still, and know that I am God; I will be exalted among the nations, I will be exalted in the earth!"
Psalm 46:10.

The fruit of coming to the quiet is finding the secret place of abiding in Him. "Come to the Quiet" means to be still. Abiding in Him is knowing He is God and learning of Him and His greatness. Do you love the secret place with Him? I forever want to dwell in the secret place where I experience knowing Him living in me, and I in Him.

So where is that place exactly? Is the secret place in the heavenly places? Or, is it inside of us? Yes, and yes. We are now His temple where He lives. Yes, you carry God, the Holy Spirit inside of you. You are the New Covenant version of the Ark of the Covenant. God has made Himself "portable." (Can I say that?) By His Holy Spirit He goes with you and is in you.

And, the omnipresent God also is seated on His most high throne in heaven. This "secret place" of Psalm 91, I believe, is the abiding that Jesus teaches us John 15. Yes, we are saved by His blood. Yes, His Spirit lives in us. Perhaps you are even filled with the Holy Spirit and move in the gifts of the Spirit. Yet, with all that, God planned even more for us. He has made it so this "abiding in Him" must also take place in our life experience so there can be kingdom-fruit in our lives on this earth—lots of fruit. And fruit is all about bringing glory to the Father (see John 15:8).

In the Parable of the Sower (Matthew 13:3-23), not all who heard the Word bore fruit. And of those who did bear fruit, their fruitfulness varied between thirty, sixty, and hundred-fold. The Master teaches us that our fruitfulness in God has everything to do with the soil that the seeds of the Word fall into. What then is this all-important "soil of our hearts"?

> "But that on the good ground are they, which in an honest and good heart, having heard the word, keep it, and bring forth fruit with patience." Luke 8:15 (also Matthew 13:23).

The Master identified our responsibility in this process of kingdom-fruitfulness. An honest and good heart is to hear and heed, or keep, His words, bringing forth fruit with patience.

> "And He said to them, "Do you not understand this parable? How will you understand all the parables?" Mark 4:13.

The kingdom key Jesus gives us in this parable, He says,

IN THE COUNSEL OF ANGELS

is the key to all the parables. We plant the seed of His Word into our good, honest soil (hearts). It is the key to fruitfulness, kingdom-effectiveness, and bringing glory to God in our lives: hearing, heeding, keeping, and bringing forth.

This "dwelling in the secret place" and "abiding in the vine" relationship with God is also evident under the Old Covenant. Elisha said it this way,

> "As the Lord of hosts lives, before whom I stand..."
> 2 Kings 3:14.

Elisha lived on the earth just like us, nevertheless he also lived with the awareness that he actually stood before God. Now that is closeness! Moses said it like this,

> "If Your presence does not go with us, do not lead us up from here." Exodus 33:15.

One day Holy Spirit said to me, "I am always in the immediate, the here and now. Meet Me there. Meet Us (meaning He and His angels) there. Pre-occupation with other things (cares, riches, pleasures) closes the door. Abandonment to Me and attentiveness to Me (heeding His word) opens the door. I am as close as your next breath. You need Me more than the next beat of your heart. The way is plain. You are in Me now, in Christ, and Christ is in you."

This "in Him" reality is not intended to be mere sound doctrine, nor just a positional truth. This "in Him" is given for us to experience as a state of living, just as Jesus experienced being "in the Father" when He walked the earth. Jesus is our prototype, our forerunner, the Way.

"The glory which You have given Me I have given to them, that they may be one, just as We are one; I in them and You in Me, that they may be perfected in unity, so that the world may know that You sent Me, and loved them, even as You have loved Me."
John 17: 22-23, NAS.

I DELIGHT TO DO YOUR WILL

> "Blessed be the God and Father of our Lord Jesus Christ, who has blessed us in Christ with every spiritual blessing in the heavenly realms." Ephesians 1:3, BSB.

How many and how diverse must be the spiritual blessings from our heavenly Father? His Word tells us we've been blessed with "every" spiritual blessing. They have all been granted to us. But have we yet seen them all? Are there more to come, waiting to be revealed? God gave Israel the Promised Land, yet they still had to go in and do what was necessary in order to possess the promise. Honestly, I have not yet seen every spiritual blessing. I am still looking to come into the possession of more of what He has promised us. How about you?

All things from God and the kingdom are received by faith.

> So that you will not be sluggish, but imitators of those who through faith and patience inherit the promises. Hebrews 6:12, NAS.

If every spiritual blessing in the heavenly realms was all meant just for heaven, then God could have just killed us when we were born again and taken us up and into those blessings. But He left us here to become the light of the world through the grace of His working; and a big part of that working is appropriating the spiritual blessings He has blessed us with.

An angel of the Lord appeared to me to instruct me in the ways of the kingdom of heaven. He said, "You have said from the heart, 'I delight to do Your will, O God.' Be aware that your delight in His will and His words to you are also permission for the Spirit to work even deeper in your heart; He is set to root out and pull down, to destroy and throw down; and yes, to build and to plant.

"And now also see that you will wield this very same power of the Spirit in your life and ministry after the Spirit has established obedience in you at this deeper, foundational level. This is kingdom multiplication. For this work of obedience to God is occurring one life at a time, and here in the one life, yours. But this word of obedience will be released through you and through others to the many, to a great many. This is kingdom authority and multiplication; the way that kingdom fruit develops. This multiplication is seen in how you all were purchased back by the blood of the One, the Christ; so that through the obedience of the One, He bought back the many. Redemption is a kingdom seed and key. It is designed with kingdom multiplication inside. All the keys of the kingdom contain kingdom multiplication. This expresses the Father's great, benevolent heart, His creation design, and His will and purpose. Now you see how wicked and twisted this world has become. Now be released from its limits. You have the key: 'I delight to do Your will, O God.' This is a part of putting on the new man, the one who is born of heaven.

"How do you think the Spirit can tell any of you of things that are beyond one's thinking and imagination? It is often done through visions and dreams. That way the natural defenses are down. Imagery can carry symbolism not

IN THE COUNSEL OF ANGELS

immediately recognized. It is like delivering a coded message that first gets by the natural defenses and is received, then decoded afterward. Peter received the vision of the unclean animals (Acts, Chapter 10); then the interpretation came. It was repeated for emphasis, and to remove doubt. Peter's vision carried a powerful, precedent-setting contradiction to cultural and religious beliefs, including Peter's own convictions, which he voices in the vision. He also yielded and chose God's will. That is revelation, obedience, and transformation at work. Not just information, but moving with the Spirit and His process on into obedience and kingdom authority.

"Now consider Mary. The message to her from the angel contradicted social law, moral law, and natural law (Luke Chapter 1). Still, she believed God's message and in so doing, she took on His interests. We are talking about active, present-tense faith.

"Now think of Abraham. He conversed with God, negotiated and even disputed with Him. God not only allowed it, He enjoyed their friendship. Remember Moses: face to face, person to person, eye to eye, mouth to mouth, and heart to heart. In that place, dark sayings and symbolism are no longer necessary. New dimensions are opening; new dimensions of heaven are coming to earth. There are those who are hearing the call in their spirit. They are being drawn to the doors of access to these dimensions. They are being drawn because they wish to hear. Many doors are opened by delighting to do His will. They open to new vistas of fresh revelation, and angelic assignments. Kingdom supplies are being delivered: material blessing, prosperity, favor with men, and the opening of doors of opportunity. It is time for cultural change. Idols will fall.

The Spirit is empowering sons and daughters to be agents of kingdom influence and cultural transformation. This is prayers being answered. This comes under the banner of, 'For the whole earth will be filled with the knowledge of the glory of the Lord, as the waters cover the sea.' And the kingdom does come in word and in power."

THE ALL-ACCESS PASS

> Through Him (Jesus) we have also obtained access by faith into this grace in which we stand, and we rejoice in hope of the glory of God. Romans 5:1-2, ESV.

Jesus is our access to God. He not only made a way for us, He *is* the way. He *is* this grace in which we stand, this gift. And He is our hope. It is all in Him and through Him. The Lord Jesus appeared to me one night and began to talk about His heart's desire: how He so wants everyone to come to Him.

He began, "God is indeed a great mystery. But I have taken away all of the mystery regarding accessing God. All of you come to Me and through Me. Draw near. Come boldly. Open the door. Everyone has been given an All-Access Pass to Me and the Father. Testify of Me. Some need a friend. Some need a healer. Some need a Lord."

I wanted to get closer to Him, so I got up and stood inside where He was in the spirit. Then He said, "To love My presence is to welcome Me. Continue to take in the new life. Soak in it. Continue to ask of Me, for access leads to power. I want all My children to come to me. Faith and trust remain your keys. I often peer in on so many of you while you sleep. I love to see you resting there. I send My angels to assist all of you. Most of you would be overwhelmed to know the details of your assignments. Trust in My Spirit leading you. I know that you

want to see the unseen realm more with your natural eyes as well, but blessed are those who having not seen, still believe."

Jesus almost laughed when He said that last sentence and that did make me laugh. He continued, "I helped Jeremiah with his qualifications. I helped Gideon with his confidence. I helped Daniel throughout his captivity. I helped Joseph ascend to his rule. Each one was made sufficient through weakness. Remember, not only because of their circumstances, but also in spite of them. The kingdom is not about getting. It is about giving out. Giving out in love is fully authorized. Whatever comes back to you is to the glory of God. To spend time with any of us (He and His angels) is also to walk in the Spirit."

Late the next night I was thinking how we all have an All-Access Pass to the kingdom; how it is as if Jesus paid for this Pass with His own blood. Just then, Jesus approached in the spirit and stood near me and asked, "Do you remember what we talked about last time?"

I said, "Yes, of course. We discussed how we all have been given an All-Access Pass to You and the Father."

He stooped by my chair and then sat on the floor. He looked relaxed but also like He was deep in thought. We sat in silence for a time. Then He looked at me and said, "I can hold a star in My hand, but I would rather spend time with any one of you."

I was thinking, "Why do You desire us so much? We are not Your equals." Of course, Jesus knew my thoughts and He said, "You are the only ones who We made in Our image. Not equal to us, but like Us and now again in Us and with Us." He reclined on the floor on one arm and got comfortable, which influenced me to relax further. Later, I realized I fell asleep

IN THE COUNSEL OF ANGELS

right after that.

In the morning as I went to my prayer spot, I saw that Jesus was again present, and right where He was last night. His presence was subtle and faint. Honestly, without consciously turning my attention to Him and applying faith I could have easily just brushed off the notion that He was present and kept on going.

I asked Him "Why do You soften Your coming to me so much?"

He had me speak in tongues for a bit, then He answered, "I want you to reach for Me with your faith. I want you all to exercise your faith. It is to your benefit, for faith is the vehicle of access. And greater faith ensures greater results. We have only just begun to emphasize faith. A faint image of Me is not a slight on your faith. I am drawing you after Me. Follow Me. Keep your eyes on Me. Do not doubt. Do not worry or even wonder. Find me in your present. Focus now on trust. Let your heart be in the present. I have so desired to be with all of you. This is it. This is who I am. We did it all for love and friendship and fellowship. You see what the evil one has done to our design. This is why the judgment against him is so severe and will be so thorough and final."

I replied, "Yes, Lord. I receive, and I believe in the 'nowness' of your presence and in the friendship of God."

So, the All-Access Pass is a way of looking at what God has provided for us all in His redemption plan through Christ; to return us to sonship, and to fellowship with Him for all eternity. It is all about God loving us and wanting us to be with Him. We are His bride and we are being changed for the wedding with Jesus. This "Way" He made for us is how He will accomplish it. God made Jesus the Way. And God is always actively engaged in His plan on our behalf in the present tense to the fullest measure imaginable, and beyond. This includes the assigning of His heavenly hosts to render service.

We have all gone to events that require you to purchase a pass or a ticket to gain entry. With some venues you can buy a Backstage Pass that may grant you access to the stars at that event. Key personnel may wear an All Access Pass, which means they are authorized to go anywhere in the venue, even into secure and exclusive areas. This is the meaning Jesus wants to get across. Through what He accomplished, He essentially purchased All Access Passes for every one of us, empowering us with the very same access to God and the kingdom of God that Jesus Himself enjoys.

Blessed be the God and Father of our Lord Jesus Christ, who has blessed us in Christ with every spiritual blessing in the heavenly realms. Ephesians 1:3, BSB.

Jesus' righteousness is forever our access to God. He tells us to "Seek ye first the kingdom of God, and his righteousness." Matthew 6:33. We approach God now in the righteousness that Jesus provides. There are not two different levels of righteousness; one for Jesus and one for us. Christ is made unto us righteousness. We are the righteousness of God in Christ. Our new man is just as right in the sight of God as Jesus, the Son. This was ensured by His blood sacrifice. We have just as much right to come to the Father as Jesus Himself does.

When that revelation touches your spirit and your heart, and you believe it, you then know that you are welcome anytime as a son or daughter of God, beloved of the Father. You have

an awakening into the heavenly identity Christ purchased and purposed for you--the new man, the heavenly one. You then begin to consciously choose to turn away from the earthly identity that is rooted only in things that originate from the earth. You begin to believe and know that the real you, your heavenly identity, is in Christ, and that you no longer need to maintain your identity that was born of this world: the old man. This is the truth about conversion. If we are tied to the identity of the man who is of earth, we are yet carnal. As our mind is renewed to live by the man that is of heaven, we begin to assume our true identity, which is the spiritual. You see that your new man has free access to God, and that you can come boldly to the throne of grace. And perhaps most importantly, you become consumed with the passion to be with Him, and to be transformed into Christ's image; for you see that He has hidden your true image in Him. You realize that your passion for Him is but a taste of the passion that God Himself has for each one of us.

Far too many Christians are still about the business of trying to make their carnal man into a good Christian. They have never left their identification with the man who is tied to earth. Enough! They need revelation from the Scripture, by the Spirit, that their new identity comes from heaven and has no relation to the carnal, earthly man, who was crucified with Christ. We are to regard ourselves as dead to our carnal man and we must no longer live in that identity of earth and flesh. This can only take place when we cease from our own works—our own efforts—to try and make things work out.

One more thing about this total access to God: the relationship goes both ways. That means you are agreeing with

God that He will now have total access to you. For Jesus wants to be Lord of our whole heart and every part of our life. His Spirit searches us. His Word makes us clean. His blood washes us. His mercy removes the weights and burdens of this life that seek to hold us down. This all is provided as we come to Him believing.

God did His part first. He gave it all. Even while we were His enemies, He loved us all the way to the cross. Now at last, we can approach Him. Now it is our turn to love Him back, by following Him, the great Lover of our souls.

TONGUES OF MEN, TONGUES OF ANGELS

If I speak with the tongues of men and of angels, but do not have love, I have become a noisy gong or a clanging cymbal." 1 Corinthians 13:1.

For one who speaks in a tongue does not speak to men but to God; for no one understands, but in his spirit he speaks mysteries, 1 Corinthians 14:2.

I thank my God, I speak with tongues more than you all. 1 Corinthians 14:18.

The following exchange with an angel opened up a door that has helped to lead me into kingdom mysteries and many new heavenly assignments as well. The angel said, "You and others have prayed to understand our purposes. We are here to tell you. You must now purpose to speak our languages at all times, even when it is inconvenient for you. To work with us is to interact with us. And a large part of interacting with us is to talk with us about the assignments and mysteries by speaking in our tongues."

These directive from the angel was accompanied by much grace. I would not presume for a moment to place this on anyone else. As stated, it came with great grace, and no burden of religious duty. Still, I would encourage any believer to

increase their speaking in tongues. When the tongue you speak is one that is attached to an angelic assignment, the angels hear it and respond to the communication between us and God. I have seen this happen many times. It is not a work of the flesh, but of the Spirit. The angels have also told me it is completely unnecessary for any of us to recognize these things as they occur. We need only be obedient to the leading and prompting of the Spirit, just as the Scriptures tell us to.

In I Corinthians 13:1, Paul states that there are languages of men and languages of angels, and he implies that he speaks those languages. I believe that tongues of men include both the organized languages of people groups, as well as (when speaking in tongues) a scrambled combining of sounds and syllables taken from many languages of men (you have likely heard people say that tongues can sound like gibberish). The devils can understand the organized languages of men. But the scrambled versions, and the languages of angels, are coded messages that the devils cannot decipher. These kinds of unknown tongues and the languages of angels are spoken on the frequencies of heaven, something that the devils have been denied access to.

Angels speak and understand both the languages of men and the languages of heaven; all the tongues of men and of angels. Or did you suppose that angels would only speak the tongues or languages of men? Angels are from heaven. Why would they speak only the languages of earth and of men? Would they not have their own heavenly languages? A "tongue" (Greek - glossa) means a "language." So of course, there are languages of the earth, and there are languages of heaven. In I Corinthians 14:2 we see that tongues are languages

IN THE COUNSEL OF ANGELS

with which we speak to God that no man understands nor comprehends. Included in these tongues that we speak to God are also the languages of heaven, the tongues of angels, for no man understands them. And so, these tongues Paul speaks of in Chapter 14 is an expanded teaching of the tongues he referenced earlier in the same letter, in Chapter 13:1.

Tongues are a powerful gift and spiritual weapon given to us by the Holy Spirit. In the book of Acts we see believers who were filled with the Spirit speaking in tongues of men and of angels, and prophesying. Speaking in tongues is an access point into the spirit realm. It is speaking mysteries to our God. This is one reason the enemy has worked so hard to sow such seeds of contention and unbelief in the church regarding speaking in tongues. In any war, it is a well-known strategy that you can weaken and even disable your enemy by severing his supply lines. Tongues are a powerful supply line given to us as a gift by the Holy Spirit. There are even godly ministers and ministerial training institutions teaching that the gift of tongues is of the devil.

The devil is no fool. He knows that any well-meaning believer would run away from practicing something that comes from him. But the Holy Spirit in His love is once again lifting the body of Christ into the doing of His will and the unity of the Spirit among believers. With this grace comes an openness of heart for all that God would bestow upon His children for the building of His kingdom in the earth.

We speak to God in tongues and we are speaking heavenly mysteries to Him

> (...but in his spirit he speaks mysteries...)

Some tongues that we speak are associated with specific angelic assignments. When Satan and his angels were cast out of heaven, they lost all access to heaven, and that includes losing access to the languages and communication frequencies of heaven. God used this idea a second time when He responded to the rebellion at the tower of Babel and sent men into disunity by confusing their communications. Just like at the Tower of Babel after God's judgment, part of the judgment on the devil and his demons for their rebellion was confusion in their communications. To this day, confusion remains one of the primary characteristics of demonic influence. The devils can no longer speak or understand heaven's languages— what is said on heaven's frequencies. It is a joy to my heart to know that the devils cannot comprehend this coded, heavenly communication between God and us; this speaking in tongues that we do to God, and that He and His angels understand.

Speaking in "unknown" tongues is a gift of the Holy Spirit.

> He said to them, "Did you receive the Holy Spirit when you believed?" And they said to him, "No, we have not even heard whether there is a Holy Spirit." And he said, "Into what then were you baptized?" And they said, "Into John's baptism." Paul said, "John baptized with the baptism of repentance, telling the people to believe in Him who was coming after him, that is, in Jesus." When they heard this, they were baptized in the name of the Lord Jesus.

> And when Paul had laid his hand upon them, the
> Holy Spirit came on them, and they began speaking
> with tongues and prophesying. Acts 19:2-6, NAS.

The Holy Spirit came on the believers, and He gave them His gift of tongues and they prophesied. Tongues are not the Holy Spirit. Tongues are one of the gifts that the Holy Spirit gives. Tongues are among the greatest of all His gifts. It is a mysterious communication from us to God; from our spirit to the One who is a Spirit.

Why is it so mysterious? Because we do not understand in our reasoning minds what we are saying to Him; but in our spirit we are speaking mysteries to Him. Speaking in tongues has been referred to as the believer's spirit language. I like that. God has given the gift of tongues to us so we can communicate with Him on the spirit-level; a level far higher and on different frequencies than our natural, reasoning minds. This is but one facet of how advanced and enhanced the communications of heaven are when compared to the communications of men. God is speaking mysteries to you. So why not speak mysteries back to God by speaking in tongues? Let the heavenly communication between you and your heavenly Father be a continuous, flowing conversation. So what if your mind is unfruitful in it? These operations are among the heavenly things; the workings of the invisible, spirit realm, and not the natural realm. They are not born of earth; they are born of heaven.

The Lord has many of you on a new path, making you forerunners and trailblazers. You are entering uncharted territories in your life experiences and in the spirit realm as a result. How could you possibly know all the

details of how to pray into your situation? Who would not want to receive into their spirit more revelation and illumination regarding the purposes of God? And you can be certain that these "purposes" include leading you further into your identity in Christ and your destiny in God; in short, the will of God for you and the good works He has prepared for you. We can pray with understanding, and thank God, we can also pray in the Spirit, in unknown tongues, where our spirits speak mysteries to our heavenly Father.

ANGELS AND MEN: ALIGNING IN THE WILL OF GOD

THE LORD AND HIS HOSTS

> O great and mighty God. The Lord of hosts is His name. Jeremiah 32:18b, NAS.

> And again, when He brings the firstborn into the world, He says, "Let all God's angels worship Him." Hebrews 1:6, ESV.

God is the Lord of Hosts (the Hebrew term is "Yahweh Sabaoth"); the God of (Angel) Armies. In the Bible, He calls Himself by this title over 300 times. Jesus Christ, the Lord of all, is Lord over His holy angels. It would fill your heart with awe to see the love and honor the angels have for Jesus, their Lord. Everything that happens with the angels happens because of the plans and commands from the Lord of Hosts, the God of Angel Armies. The ministry of angels on the earth is an integral part of the ministry of the Holy Spirit throughout the earth. For the Holy Spirit is the on-site supervisor to the hosts of heaven. Kings and rulers of the earth staff their kingdoms and governments with their servants, ministers, messengers, ambassadors, and warriors. In similar fashion God, the Lord of Hosts, has His workforce of innumerable angelic servants, ministers, messengers, ambassadors, and warriors. The Armed

IN THE COUNSEL OF ANGELS

Forces of the United States represent their Commander-in-Chief, the President of the United States. The President is head over the military, but he does not do all its work. The officers and those under their commands are absolutely essential, because they carry out the policies and orders of the Commander-in-Chief. In God's kingdom, the angels carry out the policies and orders of the Lord of Hosts, Yahweh Sabaoth. The many accounts of angelic appearances in the Bible give us a firm basis for establishing the fact that God makes use of His heavenly hosts to do His bidding. I believe we are in a time, a season, perhaps even an era, of becoming more acquainted with the reality of God's angels and their present-day working in the earth and in our lives.

The ministry of angels is front and center wherever the will of God is being carried out. This is easy to identify throughout the Scriptures. After all, what were the angels who revealed themselves doing? Were they not in every instance serving God, doing His will, and delivering His message?

> Bless the LORD, all you His hosts, you who serve Him, doing His will. Psalm 103: 21, NAS.

God created the angels and set their places within His divine order. They are His servants, His ministers, His armies, created to do His will.

Many of God's angels are enablers; they are angels who deliver heavenly resources into our lives and circumstances. These resources can range from singular events, to operations of the Spirit beyond our ability to comprehend. Think of the account in the Book of Acts where an angel came to Peter in prison and gave him safe passage by stealth, delivering him to freedom. The angel Gabriel came to Mary and announced to her the mystery and marvel of the ages, that the child she would bear as a virgin would be the Son of God. Some of these heavenly enablers abide with us, while others have more short-term assignments.

God has granted that we know and see mysteries from His heavenly realm.

> Jesus answered them, "To you it has been granted to know the mysteries of the kingdom of Heaven, but to them it has not been granted." Matthew 13:11.

In this verse Jesus said, "to know the mysteries." That word "know" is an interesting word in the Greek. It is "ginosko," and it means "to know, especially through personal experience (first-hand acquaintance)." This is experiential knowledge: knowledge gained through personally experiencing something. This is different than head-knowledge: the knowledge gained, for instance, by hearing a lecture, reading a book, or a friend telling you something. By revelation we "experience" the Spirit of Life, and the mysteries of His kingdom. It is a part of the ministry of angels to carry these mysteries and reveal them to men. We see over and over in the biblical accounts where the angels came and revealed the will of God to the person to whom God sent them. Many of the angels who are sent with a message are also here to cause that thing to happen or come to pass. This is part of the power-ministry the angels are involved in.

Acknowledging the ministry of angels is not at all the same thing as the worship of angels. When people confuse and conflate these two subjects, my observations have been that

IN THE COUNSEL OF ANGELS

it is usually due to some combination of fear, unbelief, and inexperience regarding heavenly things. The Word of God is clear: we are not to worship angels. Let us all approach God and the things of His Spirit with faith, while properly testing the spirits, and authenticating everything. As Apostle Paul instructed,

> Do not extinguish the Spirit. Do not treat prophesies with contempt, but test all things; hold fast to what is good.
> 1 Thessalonians 5:19-21.

Many people have told me they would like to see angels. I totally get it, but I believe that is in the Holy Spirit's purview. We are to seek the Lord: His love, His presence, His glory: Him! What I will often answer someone is, "Stay in the Word, and stay close with Holy Spirit. The Spirit is faithful to lead us into His will. Seek to hear from His heart and do His will. The angels will be working where Holy Spirit is working."

Angels are distinct, individual, spirit beings. How they physically appear to us may be for our earthly benefit. They have their own personality characteristics, a free will, and higher-order heavenly intelligence. They have powerful spiritual discernment; nothing in you can remain hidden or unseen to them. They know your thoughts, feelings, and intentions. There are streams of their heavenly languages where these levels of awareness and communication operate. They have also done their homework; they know your history, your circumstances, and they know in heavenly detail the plan that God has working in your life.

> For it is God who is at work in you, both to will and to

> work for His good pleasure. Philippians 2:13.

The angels deal only in truth and uprightness. As one angel said to me, "We deal only with the new man. We call forth your new man in Christ." The angels are sober and focused, but they are not gloomy. They are also witty, and can display a sense of humor, or irony. They love to dance with joy as they worship the Lord. They worship Him with a freedom and a passion that is awe-inspiring. They love to reveal your path by putting rhetorical questions to you that are full of wisdom; much the way a wise mentor might do. These types of questions may pop into your mind from time to time. Their irrefutable common sense will lead you by the wisdom of God.

It is very much part of the work of ministering angels to sometimes put thoughts in your mind; these are also the thoughts of the Holy Spirit, for they are serving Him. They speak and act on the Lord's behalf, not their own. Many people know and believe that the devils can put thoughts and suggestions into our minds. We refer to those as "attacks from the enemy." These attacks occur on the frequencies of fallen man. The devils have been locked out of the frequencies of heaven. Isn't it time for we believers to have more faith in heaven's capabilities than we have had in hell's?

Angels are regal and majestic; their very presence commands respect. They carry the holiness, the glory, and the power of God. Yet, they are clothed in humility, being remarkably selfless. Their service to God is focused on fulfilling their God-given assignments. One angel, whose job, in part, is to keep me focused on my assignment, said to me, "We are charged with

IN THE COUNSEL OF ANGELS

keeping you on your assignment. And we know how to carry out a charge." You can depend on angels to remain on task.

REVELATIONS AND MYSTERIES

"Blessed are those hungering and thirsting for righteousness, for they will be filled."
Matthew 5:6.

Jesus answered them, "To you it has been granted to know the mysteries of the kingdom of heaven, but to them it has not been granted." Matthew 13:11.

If we hunger and thirst for righteousness, we will be filled, Jesus promises us. Like all things in God's kingdom, it's a "grace" thing. We do the hungering and thirsting, and He does the filling. Learning the mysteries of the kingdom of heaven are a part of the children's bread; your portion that has been granted by Jesus, it is part of your inheritance in Him. Who in the earth should know God and the workings of His kingdom more than God's own sons and daughters? I am talking about more than just Bible knowledge that we collect with our minds. Kingdom knowledge is heart knowledge.

God's secrets are His mysteries concealed; His blessings are His treasures revealed. The above Scriptures indicate God's authorization to us to have access to His mysteries. Jesus has said we have been granted to know the kingdom's mysteries. Imagine how vast the mysteries must be of a kingdom created by Almighty God!

"Apokalupsis" is the word used in the Greek New

IN THE COUNSEL OF ANGELS

Testament for "revelation." My Greek lexicon says "revelation" means "the uncovering, unveiling, disclosure, and revealing of a thing; including its interpretation." The dictionary says that "revelation" is "the act of revealing or communicating divine truth, especially by divine agency or supernatural means." So, what is it that needs to be unveiled and revealed? It is the "musterion"; the "mysteries" of God Himself, and of His kingdom. God hides His mysteries and keeps them secret. Then, He chooses to reveal them to whom He authorizes. The Bible tells us,

> It is the glory of God to conceal a matter, but the glory of kings is to search out a matter. Proverbs 25:2.

A Greek Lexicon says of "musterion": "it is a mystery, a secret, of which initiation is necessary; and, particular truths or details of the Christian revelation." The Holy Spirit is the supernatural means by which God reveals His mysteries to us; and holy angels are God's "divine agents" whom He sends on assignments to help us.

> Are they not all ministering spirits, sent forth to minister for them who shall be heirs of salvation? Hebrews 1:14.

God loves to hide His mysteries. Our adoption as sons in Christ Jesus is our initiation into the family of God and into the unveiling of His mysteries. He hides them so He can reveal them as we seek after Him.

> "You will seek Me and find Me when you search for Me with all your heart." Jeremiah 29:13.

He has always longed for us to know Him, even as He knows us. Jesus opened the way for us to come to know Him, and the mysteries of the kingdom of heaven. This is way more than just knowing some Scriptures or religious doctrines. Jesus is talking about closeness to God. We get to actually know Him and learn from Him; learn about who He is, learn of his ways, and learn how His kingdom operates.

> "Blessed are they which do hunger and thirst after righteousness: for they shall be filled." Matthew 5:6.

We all can be filled with the knowledge of His mysteries. If we have the hunger, the Lord promises to fill us up. He is talking about becoming filled with the life of God, and of coming to know Him more and more through actual experience. When you want to get to know someone, you don't just read a book about them, or listen to someone tell you what that person is like. No. you talk with that person; you spend time with them, learning who they are, how they think, what they feel, and what they are like. Why would we think it would be that different with getting to know God? Just reading a book about God was never the point. It is about coming into a relationship with the One whom the book reveals. The Holy Spirit gives life to the Word of God. It is the glory of the Lord that transforms us into the image of Christ. We "get with the glory" because we love to be with Him, and because He changes us to become like Him.

> But we all, with unveiled face, beholding as in a mirror the glory of the Lord, are being transformed into the same image from glory to glory, just as from the Lord,

> the Spirit. 2 Corinthians 3:18, NAS.

The children of Israel maintained their distance from the Lord. As a result, they did not get to know Him but only got to observe the acts that God performed.

> He made known his ways unto Moses, his acts unto the children of Israel. Psalm 103:7.

In contrast to the rest of the children of Israel, Moses was so intimate with God that he got to know Him, even to the point that His face was shining from being in God's presence.

And the New Covenant through Jesus Christ has even more glory than God's Covenant through Moses.

> But if the ministry of death, in letters engraved on stones, came with glory, so that the sons of Israel could not look intently at the face of Moses because of the glory of his face, fading as it was, how will the ministry of the Spirit fail to be even more with glory? 2 Corinthians 3:7-8, NAS.

What is the point of hungering and thirsting for the kingdom if God doesn't have more? Our God is a big God. He is not a little god. He promised that when we do the hungering and thirsting for Him and His kingdom, He will do the filling.

THE WILL OF GOD

Bless ye the LORD, all ye his hosts (armies); ye ministers of his, that do his pleasure. Psalm 103:21, KJV.

Bless the LORD, all you His hosts (armies), you who serve Him, doing His will. Psalm 103: 21, NAS.

One day when I had entered my prayer closet to seek the Lord, it was not long before a great silence came over me from the outside. It was a peaceful stillness that filled our walk-in closet. Holy Spirit sovereignly came in His weighty presence, and it was captivating. It seemed like a peace to settle into and enjoy, so I lay down and stretched out for a long time in His presence. During that time two angels appeared and knelt by me. They both put their hands on my chest. Their presence was peaceful and intoxicating; like a holy anesthetic. One of them said, "Speak to the spirit man and not the natural man. Call the spirit man forward in people. Use the Word and the Spirit. You are acting on the Spirit's behalf, to do according to His will for them. These acts will not be of yourself. You are just His agent, working for Him. This is part of the new life He is bringing."

Notice how the Lord's messenger characterized the will of God in this instance. The angel said here that the will of God is "acting on the Spirit's behalf." And believe me, he would know.

The will of God and the activities of the angels are

IN THE COUNSEL OF ANGELS

inseparable. Everything the angels of God do is the will of God. This is what I like to call "divine alignment"; for the angels of God serve with unwavering obedience and perfect execution. (We will look at the part of "divine alignment" that pertains to man in a moment.) The above verse of Scripture tells us the work of God's angels is to "do His pleasure," which is another way of saying doing His will. Angel's wills and their work are always in perfect alignment and agreement with God's own will, because angels do not do their own wills, but they do only the will of God. By the way, the fact that the angels always do God's will is a powerful and compelling reason to listen to them when these heavenly messengers are sent to us. There are not "two wills" of God; one for man and one for angels. To be sure, the stations, roles, and functions of man are quite different than that of angels; even as the nature of man is so different from the nature of angels. Still, the working out of the will of God in our lives is integrated with the ministry of angels, for He sends them to work His will on our behalf.

> Are they (angels) not all ministering spirits, sent out to render service for the sake of those who will inherit salvation? Hebrews 1:14, NAS.

The Holy Spirit is at work in us to help us to want to do His will and the work He has for us.

> For God is the One working in you both to will and to work according to His good pleasure. Philippians 2:13.

As agents of the Holy Spirit, the angels are directly involved with this "working of God" in our lives. The Holy Spirit is our inward Helper. He is God inside us. The angels, of course, are outside of us. Angels do not replace the Holy Spirit, just like military troops do not replace their commanding officer. Rather, the troops carry out the instructions, orders, and intent (will) of their commander. The commander utilizes, directs, and positions his troops to accomplish the work and missions the commander is responsible for. Likewise, Holy Spirit utilizes His hosts, assigning and positioning them to help work out the details of His will and His missions. God reveals His will to our spirits so we may walk in the works He planned for us. The Spirit of God continues to lead us into the purposes and activities God designed specifically for each of us.

> "For we are His workmanship, created in Christ Jesus for good works, which God prepared beforehand so that we would walk in them." Ephesians 2:10, NAS.

As we learn to walk in the will of God and in these works He prepared for us, we find ourselves living in the identity of the new man in Christ Jesus. This statement works just as well expressed in the reverse: As we learn to walk in the identity of the new man in Christ Jesus, we find ourselves living in the will of God and in these works He prepared for us. The angels are present to assist and enable us in these good works, whether we know it or not, just as they are also present to help us align with God's will for us.

God prepared these good works beforehand for us, and He wrote them all down in the heavenly books (scrolls) that speak of our lives and destinies.

> Your eyes saw my unformed body; all my days were

> written in Your book and ordained for me before one of them came to be. Psalm 139:16, BSB.

The Psalm says "all your days were written in His book." I have seen some of these books and scrolls, and the angels have read to me from them. They are as prophetic as you can get, for they speak of our lives and futures as if they have already happened to us. For God, who exists outside of the limits of both time and space, those things have already been prepared and recorded as history. This is how He can call things that are not yet, as if they already were.

> Even God, who quickeneth the dead, and calleth those things which be not as though they were. Romans 4:17b.

Like God, the angels also exist outside of the natural realm and its limitations of time and space. God authorizes the angels, who live in the eternal unseen realm, to interact with and influence people and events in our natural world. As you walk in the will of God, through obedience to the revelation and wisdom of the Holy Spirit, His angels are also at work helping Him, and you, to fulfill His will and to see the good works He prepared beforehand for you become the expression of your life. This is living your life according to the divine order as written in the heavenly books. This is the part of "divine alignment" that pertains to man. This "doing of His will" is part of the process of spiritually growing towards attaining the fullness of the stature of Christ. The Master spoke of His own experience of walking in the will and the works of God when He said, "I only do what I see the Father doing." Like all things in the kingdom, this process is by grace through faith.

The learning is by doing, and the doing is by faith.

Growing in our ability to discern the will of God must certainly be one of the most important kingdom-faculties we can develop. Obedience to Him in the doing of His will assists us in cooperating with Holy Spirit and His intentions for us as we navigate through life. Our ability to know His will is designed to increase as we surrender ourselves to Him and continue to be transformed by the renewing of our minds. Surrender is first, then comes knowing.

> Therefore I urge you, brothers, on account of God's mercy, to offer your bodies as living sacrifices, holy and pleasing to God, which is your spiritual service of worship. Do not be conformed to this world, but be transformed by the renewing of your mind. Then you will be able to discern what is the good, pleasing, and perfect will of God. Romans 12:1-2.

In this instance, the offering your body to Him is the "drawing near to God" part. And, the revealing of the His will to you is the "God drawing near to you" part (see James 4:8). Ah, such sweet communion, fellowship, and friendship! This is nothing less than Jesus being "the Way" for us through the power of the Holy Spirit. You also then have ownership of this portion of your inheritance as it comes.

This revealing of God's will was so fulfilling to His inner man that Jesus declared it to be His spiritual food.

> Meanwhile, the disciples urged Him, "Rabbi, eat something." But He told them, "I have food to eat that you know nothing about." So the disciples asked one

IN THE COUNSEL OF ANGELS

another, "Could someone have brought Him food?"
Jesus explained, "My food is to do the will of Him who
sent Me and to finish His work." John 4:31-34, BSB.

Did you see it there? Jesus said the "will" and the "works." He was, of course, tuned in to God's will and the works that were prepared beforehand for Him, and now He wants the same for you and me. The knowledge of His will enters our spirit man as a revelation and as a possession, and it informs us of the work God has intended for us. Let's be careful to get the order right: we discover His will first and act on it; then comes learning about and doing the works prepared. What a waste of time and effort to try to serve God on our own. These things do not, and cannot, originate of earth or of flesh. These are heavenly things that come to us by the Spirit who has come down from heaven.

Jesus talked to Peter about the will of God for his life.

So when they had finished breakfast, Jesus said to Simon Peter, "Simon, son of John, do you love Me more than these?" He said to Him, "Yes, Lord; You know that I love You." He said to him, "Tend My lambs." He said to him again a second time, "Simon, son of John, do you love Me?" He said to Him, "Yes, Lord; You know that I love You." He said to him, "Shepherd My sheep." He said to him the third time, "Simon, son of John, do you love Me?" Peter was grieved because He said to him the third time, "Do you love Me?" And he said to Him, "Lord, You know all things; You know that I love You."
Jesus said to him, "Tend My sheep." John 21: 15-17.

Jesus handed over this heavenly charge and wisdom to one of His most-trusted apostles. He impressed upon Peter that his love for God was to be expressed in the doing of God's will and performing the good works God had prepared for him; in Peter's case, it was shepherding the people of God. As we allow Holy Spirit to align us with the doing of His will through our yielding and obedience to His Word and His leading, then the focus in our hearts and the attention of our lives shifts away from ourselves and the pursuing of our own interests. This is the key to "he who loses his life for my sake will find it." Within our heart His interests replace and become our own, and we live our life through them and through Him; thereby stepping into the marvel of living the life God designed and prepared beforehand for us. This is a facet of Christ in us, the hope of glory.

> Beloved, now we are children of God, and it has not appeared as yet what we will be. We know that when He appears, we will be like Him, because we will see Him just as He is. And everyone who has this hope fixed on Him purifies himself, just as He is pure.
> 1 John 3:2-3, NAS.

We have already stated that if you are walking in the will of God, angels are assigned to assist in that work, because the will of God is what angels do. Now I will take it a step further: If you are walking in the will of God, Holy Spirit also previously assigned angels to assist Him in getting you to that place of walking in His will. In the mind of God, our journey of salvation to glorification is one contiguous process. The Lord and His angels are at work, behind the scenes, helping

IN THE COUNSEL OF ANGELS

us in every way possible. His angels have been around us and working on our behalf longer than most of us realize. I think this is one of those "tip of the iceberg" things where we haven't seen anything yet! Walking in the will of God also illuminates the Word of God and unlocks revelation to our spirit man. Jesus said,

> "If anyone desires to do His will, he will know whether My teaching is from God or whether I speak on My own." John 7:17, BSB.

This hints at how walking in His will draws you into a special intimacy with the Master through His teachings; for the Spirit reminds us of what the Master has said and He reveals the deep things of God.

TEST THE SPIRITS BEFORE

> Beloved, do not believe every spirit, but test the spirits to see whether they are from God, because many false prophets have gone out into the world. By this you know the Spirit of God: every spirit that confesses that Jesus Christ has come in the flesh is from God; and every spirit that does not confess Jesus is not from God; this is the spirit of the antichrist, of which you have heard that it is coming, and now it is already in the world.
> 1 John 4:1-3.

This passage tells us there will be spirits that are from God and there will be spirits that are not from God. I also appreciate the clarity from the paraphrase in the New Living Testament,

> Dear friends, do not believe everyone who claims to speak by the Spirit. You must test them to see if the spirit they have comes from God. For there are many false prophets in the world.

Spiritual discernment takes place in our spirits; it is not a faculty of the natural, reasoning mind. This verse has been a reliable starting point in discerning angels and demons, and even with revealing the hidden motives of the human heart, both good and bad.

Test the spirits (and also, motives) before you choose to

IN THE COUNSEL OF ANGELS

listen to them. We need to determine whether they are from God. Test them before you listen; do not wait until during, and certainly not after, you listen. Demonic spirits are often subtle and intrusive. They like to get us to think that their thoughts are actually our thoughts. Demons are toxic, as are their demonically influenced thoughts, emotions, and motives. Once the demon-influenced thought is given access to someone's mind, that person will suffer some trouble as a result. Then measures will need to be taken to correct and clean up the mess. So, call it testing, screening, filtering, or whatever; testing is what we do.

Developing spiritual discernment is a growth process. Before we are of much use in helping others discern things, we must learn to test and discern the input that comes to our own selves. We must learn to protect our own "castle" through spiritual discernment. Try not to get down on yourself when you've messed up and let the enemy through your defenses. We pick ourselves up, dust ourselves off and go again, always seeking the Spirit's help. In our own lives we are to learn to do the testing of our thoughts, feelings, and desires; all the areas of our souls. That is why we learn to follow the Word of God and the Spirit of God. Basic spiritual discernment is developed with intent and through Holy Spirit's process over time. Holy Spirit will initiate special training processes when He wants to develop advanced spiritual discernment in

> DEVELOPING SPIRITUAL DISCERNMENT IS A GROWTH PROCESS. WE MUST LEARN TO PROTECT OUR OWN "CASTLE" THROUGH SPIRITUAL DISCERNMENT.

us as an equipping for some ministry emphasis. Note how a professional athlete will condition and train his or her body through systematic and consistent training to prepare for competing at a high level. Do not try to rush the development of your spiritual discernment. It will happen through practice. Trust Holy Spirit for His process, and especially believe in His love and grace. He has raised many spiritual children.

> For everyone who partakes only of milk is not accustomed to the word of righteousness, for he is an infant. But solid food is for the mature, who because of practice have their senses trained to discern good and evil. Hebrews 5:13-14, NAS.

We have the choice to test. We have the choice to listen. We have the choice to believe. Holy Spirit's wisdom is pure, peaceable, gentle, and unambiguous. The Spirit will not attempt to throw us off balance or override our will. Demons, on the other hand, by nature are deceptive, manipulative, controlling, and enticing. Lies, seduction, traps, subtlety, guilt, and uncleanness are all hallmarks of demonic spirits. Incidentally, if someone is not living a holy and clean life before the Lord, it will be next to impossible for them to recognize unclean spirits when they come to tempt. Get the first things first: run to Jesus! His blood will wash you clean. He will lift you up. He will set your feet upon the Rock of Himself.

First, test the spirit. Ask "Has Jesus Christ come in the flesh?" Then either approve of or reject that spirit. I cannot overstate the importance of the order. It is like an "early warning system" put in place by God for our safety. Angels of God readily accept and submit to this testing. This has proven

IN THE COUNSEL OF ANGELS

to be true for me countless times. If approved of with this Scriptural test and with peace from the Holy Spirit, then and only then do I proceed to listen to what they have to say. Even while they speak, I continue to test everything with the Word and the Spirit. We are to be Spirit-led, Word-stabilized, and love-rooted. This is especially important when ministering to someone who is under the influence of ideas, beliefs, behaviors, or spirits that are contrary to Christ. Your spirit is constantly testing, filtering, discerning. This type of spiritual discernment is a realm apart from the reasoning of the natural mind, with its earth-bound perspectives of criticism and suspicion. The spiritual mind and the natural mind receive and transmit on completely different frequency ranges.

Demonic spirits often conceal themselves, preferring to remain disguised or behind the scenes. But, no matter how they and their work appear to look or sound outwardly, they cannot disguise or cover-up their rebellious nature and spirit as they assert themselves. Therefore we must discern the inner nature of a thing and not believe every spirit that comes along. As one of God's angels explained to me, "The devils cannot operate on our frequencies (the frequencies of heaven and of God's holiness). They no longer have access to them. But they do operate on the same frequencies as the souls of fallen men and the flesh. That is where you will detect them. It is also where temptation and deception come in."

The devils use these frequencies to come and try to tempt us in the areas of our minds, wills, and emotions. Jesus revealed this kingdom mystery and key to us in this passage,

> And He began to teach them, that the Son of man

must suffer many things, and be rejected of the elders, and of the chief priests, and scribes, and be killed, and after three days rise again. And He spoke that saying openly. And Peter took Him, and began to rebuke Him. But when He had turned about and looked on His disciples, He rebuked Peter, saying, Get thee behind me, Satan: for thou savors not the things that be of God, but the things that be of men." Mark 8:31-33.

Satan was able to tempt Peter because Satan operates in the realm (on the same fallen frequencies) of the natural thoughts, feelings, and desires of men. What Peter thought was his compassion towards Jesus, the Lord instead discerned that it was actually the ploy of satan. The devil deceived Peter and used him as a vehicle to attack Christ in direct opposition to the very will of God for our Savior. Since Peter did this in front of the others, Jesus rebuked him openly for all to see. I feel bad for Peter here; but I thank the Master for His lesson on discernment.

DISCERNMENT: SEEING THROUGH TO WHAT IS HIDDEN

But solid food is for the mature, who because of practice have their senses trained to discern good and evil.
Hebrews 5:14, NAS.

There was a man who in a dream was given power to change and color some of the objects in the world around him. In this dream an angel stood before the man. All around them, the things on earth were only outlined in black; plants, trees, cars, buildings, people. And all these things were colored inside the black outlines in only white. It was like a coloring book waiting to be colored in. The angel said to the man, "I will now teach you something about discernment with a simple test." The angel held up in one hand a sheet of colored paper. He asked the man, "What color do you see?"

The man replied, "I see a shade of the color green."

Then the angel asked the man, "What things of earth around us might be the color you see on the paper?"

The man responded, "Many of the plants and trees are shades of green."

"Yes, of course," said the angel. "Now, if you are certain, command that it be done in the color you are seeing on the paper."

And so the man said, "Let the plants and trees around us

become the color I am seeing on the paper."

Instantly the plants and trees all became blue. The man was taken aback, and he asked the angel, "What happened? What went wrong?"

The angel brought his other hand up to the sheet of paper. With one hand he removed from the front a sheet of color-tinted plastic transparency, while still holding a sheet of paper in his other hand. This revealed that there had been two separate sheets: a sheet of blue-tinted plastic transparency, in front of a sheet of paper colored opaque yellow. The angel said, "The first sheet is see-through blue; the second sheet is solid yellow. You were looking at the blue sheet without actually seeing it. Neither did you recognize the yellow sheet behind the blue one. Your eyes could not distinguish the two sheets or their individual colors. You only saw them as one. From your wrong seeing you then formed a wrong conclusion. And from your wrong conclusion, you then made a wrong decision and acted on it; all the while believing you were correct. Then you saw that you made all the plants and trees blue, though you thought you were making them green. What went wrong?"

The man replied, "The information I had was incomplete, and so my judgment was mistaken. I did not have enough information to make the correct decision."

"Exactly. There was no green among the two separate elements and your sight was unable to recognize this. Your judgment was based on a convincing illusion.

"And so it often is with people's judgment of things—their discernment is incomplete and their decisions are premature. Before all things are properly separated into their elements and then discerned individually, you may risk making an inaccurate judgment, all the while believing you got it right. A great many errors in this world are caused by this very thing. People will even insist that they are right, and fight for it."

The man questioned the angel, "But how could I have known there was more there than I could see?"

The angel replied, "We are talking about seeing through layers, seeing more than meets the eye, even seeing behind things that are hidden. This works with good and with evil. This kind of spiritual discernment only comes through constant practice. This is kingdom growth. It is an invitation to come closer to Him. It is a part of your inheritance as His sons."

EAT YOUR PROPHECIES

> This charge I commit unto thee, son Timothy, according to the prophecies which went before on thee, that thou by them mightest war a good warfare; holding faith, and a good conscience; which some having put away concerning faith have made shipwreck. 1Timothy 1:18-19, KJV.

One day an angel delivered this lesson to me, "Too many people do not know what to do with the prophecies they receive. They carry them around and talk about them, as if waving them in the air, showing them off for a time, and then toss them aside like a child tired of a toy. Then they seek another prophecy, having never put to proper use the previous one. You are to eat your prophecies. They are food for your spirit man. They are to become part of you. And like the loaves and fishes, the revelations can open up and multiply as you continue in them."

If someone received a wrapped gift, who would just wave it in the air and tell everyone they received a gift, and then toss it aside without ever having opened it? What a waste! But that is the picture the angel gave of what some have done with prophecies given to them, not understanding how to properly treat them. True prophecies confirm the Lord's work in our lives and carry the kingdom authority to take us further. So, "eat your prophecies" means that we are to believe from the

IN THE COUNSEL OF ANGELS

heart the prophecies the Spirit gives to us.

Yes, we do judge and evaluate prophesy to determine its veracity. It is a good idea even to consult with our spiritual overseers to help with discerning a prophetic word. True prophecies are a ministry of the Holy Spirit and will contain wisdom and revelation, even preparing us for what is to come.

> "But when He the, Spirit of truth, shall come, He will guide you into all the truth. For He will not speak from Himself, but whatever He may hear, He will speak. And He will declare to you the things coming."
> John 16:13.

Prophecy is both an offensive and defensive spiritual weapon for the battles that lie ahead. "By them you might wage the good warfare." Receiving a true prophecy requires that we put faith to action. Like the loaves and fishes, the revelations can open up and multiply. True prophecy is a living word from the Spirit, both powerful and precious.

> Earnestly pursue love and eagerly desire spiritual gifts, especially the gift of prophecy. 1 Corinthians 14:1, BSB.

Prophecy is a great gift to have and it's great to be ministered to by someone with an accurate gift of prophecy. But as with all ministry gifts, good fruit is born of good character. A solid personal character and good personal fruit are a must for your life's foundation.

NEW TONGUES FOR NEW REALMS

> "These signs will accompany those who have believed: in My name they will cast out demons, they will speak with new tongues." Mark 16:17.

The unseen spirit realm is vast beyond all human comprehension. There are many dimensions to it; in fact, there are a great many realms within the all-encompassing spirit realm. In the earth there are many kingdoms; many territories, all of which are ruled by some form of government. In the spirit realm there are many territories, all of which are ruled over by a territorial sovereign. The dictionary says a "realm" is "a territory over which a sovereign rules; a kingdom." Also, it is "an area or sphere of activity." Jesus is Lord of all; which means He is the rightful Sovereign Ruler over all the heavenly realms and the natural realm. Christ defeated sin by the shedding of His blood and with His death on the cross. His resurrection from the dead demonstrated that He defeated death itself and openly showed He defeated Satan and all of the demons. The glorified Christ later said to John the Beloved,

> "I am the first and the last, and the living One; and I

PROPHECY IS BOTH AN OFFENSIVE AND DEFENSIVE SPIRITUAL WEAPON FOR THE BATTLES THAT LIE AHEAD.

IN THE COUNSEL OF ANGELS

> was dead, and behold, I am alive forevermore, and I have the keys of death and of Hades."
> Revelation 1:17-18 NASB.

Without a doubt, Jesus holds the keys to every realm of authority. And He turns to His followers—His church—and He delegates His authority to us.

> "I also say to you that you are Peter, and upon this rock I will build My church; and the gates of Hades will not overpower it. I will give you the keys of the kingdom of heaven." Matthew 16:18-19, NAS.

Jesus said we would speak with new tongues (or "languages"). The word "new" or "kainós" in the Greek means: new in quality (innovation), fresh in development or opportunity, and "not found exactly like this before." Other meanings and renderings include: "recently made, fresh, unused, unworn, of a new kind, unprecedented, novel, uncommon, unheard of."

Clearly, the verse is not referring to speaking earthly languages, as those languages are already known and spoken. Jesus is telling us about speaking in new and heavenly languages, the tongues of angels. We have already discussed that these "tongues" are our spirit language with which we speak to God. There are many, many heavenly languages and dialects of angels; far more than the number of languages and dialects of men.

Let's take a closer look. Do the tongues you speak in often sound familiar, like tongues you've spoken in before? Many people would say, "Well, yes." Why do you suppose that our spirit language sounds so familiar much of the time, especially when Jesus said we would speak in new tongues? When you first spoke in tongues, certainly that was new tongues to you at the time. But can there continue to be new tongues open to us? Do you think you already speak all the angel languages? I suspect that many of us may still speak mostly with the tongue we received when we first spoke in tongues. I believe that first tongue or language is most often the giving of thanks to God in the Spirit.

> Otherwise if you bless in the spirit only, how will the one who fills the place of the ungifted say the Amen' at your giving of thanks, since he does not know what you are saying? For you are giving thanks well enough, but the other person is not edified. I thank God, I speak in tongues more than you all.
> 1 Corinthians 14:16-18 NAS.

Paul says here, "When you bless" and "When you give thanks" in the spirit (in tongues. That is our first spiritual language; it is the giving of thanks to God. And it is very important.

> Enter into his gates with thanksgiving, and into his courts with praise: be thankful unto him, and bless his name.
> Psalm 100:4 KJV.

Our entry into His presence includes having a thankful heart from which flows thanks and praise. It is true with our human tongues, and it is duplicated with our spiritual tongues. So clearly, this is a good thing.

Now let's build on this understanding of tongues. Speaking with these new tongues, new spiritual languages—fresh, innovative, unheard of spiritual languages—is a direction we

IN THE COUNSEL OF ANGELS

want to head in, because Jesus, Lord of the church and Head of the body said we would. We still allow Holy Spirit to lead us in this.

An angel from the Council shared with me some fresh understanding of the workings of the kingdom of heaven. He said, "Assignments into new realms are ready for distribution in great numbers. Your entry into these realms will be accompanied by guardians. Tongues should increase now. New tongues should be sought and found; new tongues for new realms. I told you new realms are entered by faith." God's angel affirm Christ's words, and opens this kingdom mystery; we are to seek to speak to God with new tongues that we might align with His will and move in the Spirit into new realms of gifting, assignments, operations, authority, and yes, new angelic involvement, for we will be speaking their languages.

Let me say it a different way. Do you think that speaking in tongues should be limited to only thanking and praising God? As good and as necessary as that is, isn't there far more to being about our Father's business? Have you prayed that He would show you new areas of His will in your life, your ministry, or in the lives of others? Do you want to see a fresh move of God in your life, your city, your nation, other nations? Do you want to see God working in and through you in new ways that brings glory to Him and reveals His kingdom on earth? If you want to interact with the Lord and intelligently engage with His resources in the heavenly realm, then speak to Him in heaven's languages, spirit to Spirit. By faith, speak in new tongues, asking the Spirit to help you.

Now let's make it practical. God will engage you at your level of surrender and build from there. I am talking about speaking new sounds, new words, and new phrases in tongues that you have never heard before. Do you remember when you first got this gift from the Holy Spirit, this "speaking in tongues"? Some people say it sounded like baby-talk, or gibberish; even like they were just making it up. I don't care if you've been saved forty or fifty years or more; stepping out to speak in a new tongue for the first time may again sound like gibberish to your natural mind. But you will soon realize that a whole new vista of prayer and activation in the spiritual realm has been opened to you. This is something I believe He wants to do. By grace through faith, it is the Holy Spirit who gives utterance. I now pray in tongues almost all the time; this includes new tongues I've never heard before. It's not a badge of religious accomplishment; it's a grace thing, through faith. It just grew and grew, and sort of happened.

Seek for and find these new tongues, then speak mysteries to God that He might speak mysteries back to you, growing you in your calling in Christ. Knock on this door that it might open. Fresh revelation will flow from God's heart to yours. Your yielding to Him allows Him to set you on fire. In many ways I feel this is the most important topic in this whole book. For me, these new tongues have been the door that opened communications with heaven; the angelic assignments, the fresh awareness of and closeness to the Lord, and of His call and destiny in my life. But it is always by grace, in the rest that is by faith, not by self-effort.

I'll issue a disclaimer here: "Caution. Results may vary." We do not want to try to be like anyone else. That is a bad trail to go down. As always, we want to yield to the Lord, discern where He chooses to take us, and follow His lead.

SNAPSHOTS OF THE UNSEEN

HEAVENLY EYES AND EARS

The eyes of the LORD are upon the righteous, and his ears are open unto their cry. Psalm 34:15

This final section contains some encounters with the unseen realm that are a bit shorter, and a little more on the lighter or humorous side. Angels live in the eternal realm of heaven; the place where we too now are alive through Christ. It is such an amazing and lively place! As the saying goes, "You never know what to expect next!"

Our church, Westside Vineyard, was hosting an event called "Accelerate Prophetic School" put on by Father's House Ministries, Portland, Oregon. On the first day of this seminar, while still at our home, my wife saw in the spirit a gathering of large angelic eagles circling above the Westside church property. She said they were hovering and brooding, a sign of a prophetic birthing in the spirit. Scores of people from all over the region were in attendance for the seminar. During one of the worship sessions I saw a portal open to the spirit realm just above the church. The opening was round and must have been about sixty feet across. The rim of the portal was lined entirely with perched large eagle angels and large hawk angels.

These angelic being are enablers; spirits of revelation and entreaty, who operate closely with believers. Holy Spirit let me watch and listen in as two of the angelic eagles talked together.

The first eagle said to the other, "They are doing really well."

The second eagle replied, "You realize they have no idea of the great things coming?"

The first eagle answered, "Yes, they will be beyond amazed. For many, their grids will be blown. But they are obedient and will rise with it."

"I know. Just look how they use His joy to war with."

I figured I would just continue to listen in on their discussion. But right then, the first eagle looked down, right at me looking up at him, and he said to me, "You can tell them, if you like." It really shocked me when he spoke directly to me. I thought I had been watching the eagle angels in a vision, but instead, it was a visitation; an actual angelic encounter in real-time. These powerful angelic creatures were there on assignment and were ready to render service and minister to us. Heaven's eyes and ears are always close by.

ARMY IN MY PRAYER CLOSET

> Then Elisha prayed and said, "O LORD, I pray, open his eyes that he may see." And the LORD opened the servant's eyes and he saw; and behold, the mountain was full of horses and chariots of fire all around Elisha.
> 2 Kings 6:17, NAS.

This visitation occurred very early in the new assignment the Lord placed on me. You will notice the level of surprise I experienced, and this underscores how moving it has been to gradually grow more accustomed to the spirit realm in general, and angelic activity in particular. The Lion Angel General and my Lead Angel presented themselves while I was in my living room. They wanted me to go up to my prayer closet. They were already there when I arrived. I knelt before the Lord and spoke in tongues for a while. My tongues seemed to change languages every few phrases. My attention shifted, because I sensed an overwhelming presence with me, above me, and around me; very similar to having many, many sets of eyes looking at you. Then the Lion Angel said, "We are here."

As he spoke those words, I could see an uncountable heavenly host gazing down at me from above, like we were in a giant amphitheater rising UP into the sky. I was powerfully impacted by this revelation. I could feel the presence of these angelic beings, like energy raining down upon me. I did not know how to express the reaction I was experiencing. All at once a variety of different emotions moved through me; there was wonder and amazement, a sense of smallness, alarm, even unworthiness. I began to laugh and cry, and sway and stoop, all at the same time. Goose bumps were all over my body. I even became nauseous. I cried out, "Lord, what are you doing with me?"

"Now you will be changed," the Lion Angel answered kindly. The angels are full of the love of God for His people. They minister to us, fight for us, and protect us. He continued, "React neither to the awe, nor the unbelief of people. That is not your mission. We are bringing heaven down to the church. Get ready."

PUSHED BY AN ANGEL

> For He will give His angels charge concerning you; to guard you in all your ways. They will bear you up in their hands, that you do not strike your foot against a stone. Psalm 91:11-12, NAS.

This is the story of the time when an angel pushed me off the stage at church. He then bore me up in his hands, and that stunt healed my leg!

Before I tell the story, you need some background information. For over five years prior to this event I had lived with a knot nearly the size of a walnut in my left calf muscle. One day I had helped a guy push his dead car off the road, and I pulled the calf muscle in my left leg in the process. All my efforts over months to stretch that muscle and get rid of the knot had been unsuccessful. It was not very painful to live with, but it did slightly limit the range of motion in my ankle. Really, I had all but forgotten about it; life must go on.

Now for the rest of the story. It was a few minutes before the morning service at our church was to begin. I went up on stage to speak a blessing to the worship team, like I sometimes do. The stage platform is elevated about twelve inches higher than the sanctuary floor. As I spoke a blessing to various worship team members, I also sensed a strong angelic presence and activity in the area. My eyes were closed, and I began

IN THE COUNSEL OF ANGELS

jumping straight up and down mimicking the angels' actions of praising God. I was not near anyone at that moment, and I was a full eight feet away from the edge of the stage platform. Suddenly, I had the sense of rapid sideways motion. I opened my eyes and to my surprise I was still jumping, but I was now also moving sideways very fast and towards the front edge of the stage. It happened so fast there was no time to slow down my momentum and I knew I was about to fly off the stage sideways while being airborne. I was hoping I could land on my feet without falling and injuring myself. The right side of my body left the stage first, but I landed on my left leg. The left leg took the load and it immediately gave out; my right leg did not plant to stop my momentum, but somehow I came to an immediate halt and remained standing. Instantly I could not put any weight on that left leg. It was very painful and there was no strength in the knee. I locked my knee and walked stiff-legged and in pain back to my seat. The usual thoughts were going through my mind, like you would have when you injure yourself, especially right in front of a room-full of people. But there were also a few thoughts in my mind which were not so usual. Like, "Did something just push me off that stage? And, did something catch me and keep me from falling down?" But I knew it was not some "thing"; it was some "one."

I asked the Holy Spirit, "Why did your angel just push me off the stage while I was worshipping the Lord with them?" I did not hear any answer back.

I could not walk on that leg for the next two days, unless I kept my left knee locked, and rotated the leg only at the hip, like an old peg-legged pirate. There was no muscle support behind my knee. It had no strength for load bearing at all; only

pain. After a few more days the leg began to recover. I reached down to feel the area, wondering if I had torn anything. As I felt my left calf muscle, it was all soft and pliable. There was no knot remaining in the muscle at all, anywhere! I tested my left foot for range of motion and found that it had regained its full range of normal motion, and without pain. Everything was back to normal. Wow!

It was all a set-up. The angel (or angels) and the Holy Spirit orchestrated the whole thing. I was pushed off the stage by an angel and healed as that very awkward landing obviously stretched the knot right out of my calf muscle. Praise God. As I thought this through, I came to realize that an angel also caught me after the jump (maybe even the same angel) and instantly stopped my momentum. You remember the verse,

> The steps of a good man are ordered by the Lord.
> Psalm 37:23.

I'll bet you've never heard it applied quite like that before! What planning it took. They had calculated my body weight, the distance, and angle of the fall, the tightness of the knot in my muscle, the velocity needed and the exact amount of contact pressure on my left foot necessary to stretch my calf muscle and free it of that knot, all without creating further injury. Then they just waited, until I got in position on the stage that day; eyes closed and leaping up and down in praise to God. They then pushed me and caught me; and made sure my weight came down on the left leg.

> They (the angels) shall bear thee up in their hands, lest thou dash thy foot against a stone. Psalm 91:12.

My leg was healed. Talk about ministering spirits! How amazing is our God who watches over and cares for us? Has something like that happened to you or someone you know? I have heard other stories of body repairs happening to people in similar outrageous fashion. God is so creative, so caring, and so good!

MY PASTORS AND THE SPIRIT REALM

> When they had finished eating, Jesus asked Simon Peter, "Simon son of John, do you love Me more than these?" "Yes, Lord," he answered, "You know I love You." Jesus replied, "Feed My lambs."
> John 21:15, BSB.

The care for the flock of God by the spiritual overseers of our local church is exemplary. They are all wonderfully gifted men and women who are dedicated and caring servants of the Lord. Our preachers consistently dig deep into the Word and the things of the Spirit. You would be hard-pressed to find more anointed teaching and preaching anywhere. It is so encouraging to me when I see the ways Holy Spirit causes the spirit realm to interact with our pastors. Here are a couple of fun snippets.

I had lunch with Pastor Micah and his son and daughter on a certain day. The Black Panther Throne had appeared to me while at their house, and I shared that with them over lunch. Pastor Micah later wrote me a note about what he experienced that afternoon after he went back to the church office. He wrote, "I still don't know what to make of it really but just by way of confirming, I went back to my office after our lunch and did a few things but I think I actually fell asleep or was at least almost passed-out for a couple hours. I was just drained; I don't know how else to describe it. I know it had no purely natural explanation; it was a distinctly spiritual phenomenon. I have to say I hope it isn't the main way angels are going to be making me aware of their presence, but it certainly provides another level of evidence for me of what you're sharing." Sounds to me like an angelic presence was nearby, all right! Maybe even an angelic Black Panther?

One time at church I was standing at my seat next to the center aisle. Pastor Arlan was standing at the front, praying and beginning to lead us into the ministry time. My eyes were closed when I felt someone nudge my arm as they walked by; not just brush it, but a nudge that moved my arm and shoulder, as you might do if you were trying to get someone's attention. I opened my eyes but there was no one walking there, even close by. So I looked in the spirit and I saw it was the Lord Jesus who had just walked past, playfully shoulder-bumping me to say "Hello" as He passed by. This was His way of getting me to watch what was coming next. I watched Him as He continued walking forward towards the front of the sanctuary. Jesus got within six feet of Pastor Arlan, whose eyes were closed, just as he said, "Jesus is here, and walking among us."

If you were to ask my pastor if he sees in the spirit, he would likely tell you that his sensing in the spirit is more developed. I can assure you his sensing in the spirit is perceptive and accurate.

This one happened also at the beginning of prayer ministry time during the evening service. Pastor Arlan was on the stage and leading us in corporate prayer. I saw two messenger angels descend onto the stage, just behind and on either side of where the pastor was standing. One angel carried a short scepter-like cut crystal that shone with light. The other angel held a scroll. The pastor paced back and forth across the stage a few times. He stopped right in front of the angel who had the scroll and was facing away from the angel and towards the congregation. The pastor put his hands out in front of him with palms upward and fingers partly curled. The angel reached over the pastor's back and placed the scroll in his hands, which were already perfectly positioned to receive it. Just then, the Spirit said to me, "The next thing the pastor says has just come from the Father's mouth and is written on the scroll." Immediately, Pastor said these words: "Give place to the Holy Spirit and receive Him. It is the Father actively showing His love for us."

HEAVENLY ANOINTING OF A PROPHET'S WORDS

During our Kingdom Ministry Class one evening, a visiting minister and friend, a man of God and a prophet, was just about ready to take the microphone and share with us what was on his heart. Suddenly, in the spirit I saw six angels drop down out of the sky and land on the stage, just behind the man of God. Standing in a perfect line, each angel raised his right arm sending it back over his shoulder, positioning the palm of his hand flat and facing up. Then from behind each of the angels, an arm appeared with a loaf of flatbread in its hand and a loaf was placed in each angel's raised hand. In unison the six angels leaned forward and slapped their loaves down onto the stage. Each loaf had steam rising from it. Then the angels returned to their standing position and one said, "Fresh bread from heaven is served." The declaration from heaven revealed by this vision demonstrated that they had joined us in that meeting, depositing the anointing of the Spirit for the Word of God about to be preached.

ANGELS' WINGS

> Keep me as the apple of Your eye; Hide me under the shadow of Your wings. Psalm 17:8, NKJ.

I was with one of our church's intercessor teams meeting at a member's home. We were soaking in worship music as we sought the Lord together in silent meditation, also known as contemplative prayer. I saw in the spirit a large Hawk Angel, who descended and began hovering just above us. He would flap his wings; not for flying, but to release an impartation.

A powerful sense of the peace and assurance of God was being released upon us. I listened to hear the angel's message. The silent language coming from his spirit said, "Layers. He comes to you in layers. He does not give and then take it back. He is not a man. His ways are not like the ways of men. The ways of the kingdom are higher than the ways of men. He continues to come with the ways of the kingdom. He is a giver. He adds to you by layers, one after another, after another. This is another elevation of His purposes upon you all. Be consumed in His purposes. Cleansing, purging, purifying, liberating; building identity, hearts full of thanks, lives surrendered to the care of His love.

"The spoils of victory are being handed out. Sound out the notice. Come to the table and eat. The Great Giver has prepared a table for you, even in the presence of your

IN THE COUNSEL OF ANGELS

enemies. Now resolve to come higher in your faith, for He has determined that you would continue to rise. Can you take more blessing? The anointing oil starts at the head, and quickly runs down onto the body. The body has not known anointing oil like this. You've seen it on individuals, but many have thought they would never know it upon themselves. His anointing is full of His love. Open up to it. His anointing over you is love. Do not be afraid of His power when it comes. It is also borne of His love.

"There will be joy explosions; explosions of joy. Joy because of the liberty He gives. Joy in experiencing His matchless love. Joy because He is joyful. To know Him is to serve Him. Here comes

> HE MADE YOUR DEPTHS FOR HIMSELF, THAT HE WOULD LIVE THERE. HEAR IT: HE MADE THE DEPTHS OF YOU SO HE COULD LIVE THERE, IN YOU AND WITH YOU.

deeper truths, and also truth going deeper into your being; even to the depths where you live, the depths you cannot access on your own. But His Spirit can access them. He made your depths for Himself, that He would live there. Hear it: He made the depths of you so He could live there, in you and with you. You are to actually become filled with all His fullness.

"Now comfort His people for your bondage has ended, and your Deliverer is great. He is mighty. He is the Lord, mighty in battle; full of compassion, full of mercy. He is also your Great Lover, and your Eternal Reward. He fulfills His Word. He fulfills His promises. He cannot be shaken. He cannot be moved. And what He wills is what He will do. Comfort yourselves in this."

ANGELS WINGS

See the angels in flight, borne by the Sovereign's might.
His Spirit is the very wind by which they have flown.
See them as they stir their wings, releasing heavenly things.
His presence and His glory, sent out from His throne.

TURN ASIDE AND SEE?

Now Moses was tending the flock of Jethro his father-in-law, the priest of Midian. And he led the flock to the back of the desert, and came to Horeb, the mountain of God. And the Angel of the LORD appeared to him in a flame of fire from the midst of a bush. So he looked, and behold, the bush was burning with fire, but the bush was not consumed. Then Moses said, "I will now turn aside and see this great sight, why the bush does not burn. So when the LORD saw that he turned aside to look, God called to him from the midst of the bush and said, "Moses, Moses!" And he said, "Here I am."
Exodus 3:1-4, NKJ.

One of the angel Counselors probed my heart when he asked me one day, "Can God ask a man or a woman to become something they have not been? Would He do that? Has He done it before? Then why not do it again? Why not now? How could He cause someone's life to be to the praise of His glory if He didn't make them into someone whom they had not been naturally? How far will you reach? How much faith will you have? There is no middle ground here. There is only 'yes' or 'no,' and then you move along that path. There is only the way of David who yielded to God, or the way of Saul who disobeyed Him.

"The unlimited greatness of the Father's gifts, His graces, is because of His nature and the greatness of His heart. The gifts are not portioned-out based on one's natural abilities, lineage, or because of something one might think they deserve. God's gifts are given freely. It is according to His grace: His unfettered love for us, His election, His wisdom, and His will. His purpose for each of you unfolds according to His plans. Look for His working in your lives along the lines of what He has promised you. To do this it must be the looking that is by faith, and not by the looking that evaluates according to observable circumstance. This is also the drawing near to Him, and the minding of heavenly things.

"Who will open their spirit to the greatness of the possibilities of faith in all that your heavenly Father has granted to you, planned for you, and is ready to release in you?"

Are you prepared for Him to reveal His appointed time to you? He is poised to give to us from His bounty, far more even than we want to receive it.

When He comes who will know to "turn aside and see" like Moses, and answer God's call? Insert your name here:

And now say, "Yes Lord, here I am."

NOT "THE END," BUT "MORE LORD."

AFTERWORD

For reasons that are His own, the Lord Jesus has seen fit to have me live and work on the eighth mountain, the mountain of the house of the Lord, working very closely with Holy Spirit and many of His angels. My assignment is very specific and ever-expanding. Part of that work includes reporting back to you, His bride, on what I have seen and heard. This is the nature and content that has filled my book.

Blessings to all you, His servants, and beloved sons, as we seek and work and watch His kingdom come, His will be done, on earth as it is in heaven. All glory be to His wonderful, matchless Name.

~Bob Blase (Micah 4:1, Heb. 12:22-24.)

ABOUT THE AUTHOR

Bob Blase is an ordained minister, intercessor, and seer-prophet who attends and serves at Westside Vineyard Church in Portland, Oregon. Several years ago the Lord began sending angels to visit Bob during his prayer times. The Lord now has the angels bring him assignments and revelations about His purposes locally and elsewhere. Bob works with his pastors and other local ministers to identify and align with Holy Spirit's angelic activities and operations. These activities include angelic messages, spiritual warfare, seeing into the unseen realm, spiritual mapping, and teaching on demystifying the spirit realm.

ARTWORK

SKETCHES
"Praying and listening to worship music plus hearing promptings of the Holy Spirit while I'm painting and drawing seems to work well for the worship art. I give Holy Spirit all the glory for the images we produce together."

~Marv Watkins letheavenspeak.com

COVER
Cover created and designed by Pelton Media Group, Portland, Oregon.

INSCRIBE PRESS

Incribe Press was formed to publish literary prophetic works that ignite the fires of wholenss and holiness in readers. Through our publishing house and training programs, we encourage and inculcate human creativity and diversity; qualities which display the majesty and versatility of our Creator, whose very essence is the fountain of all beauty and truth.

Beauty is vital for human flourishing as we walk in humility and love with God. Truth is not nebulous or subjective; it is objective and universal and, rightly lived out, it sets us free.

If you would like more information about opportunities for publishing your work, or to learn more about honing your craft and walking in the calling of an artist, please write us at admin@inscribepress.com.

www.ingramcontent.com/pod-product-compliance
Lightning Source LLC
Chambersburg PA
CBHW020137130526
44591CB00030B/98